Alan Hester has managed at all levels from team leader to director in a career taking in the public, community and private sectors. In 2002 he formed Alan Hester Associates, delivering practical, interactive workshops for leaders and managers. His passion is about working with delegates to increase their confidence and resilience, helping them to see that the results they achieve are a direct result of their attitude, skills and knowledge. His approach to writing this book is the same, and in it he distils some of the most powerful insights and approaches that make his courses so popular and effective.

Hester lives with his wife, Eunice, in Berkshire. They have a son, Michael, and a daughter, Charlotte, two cats and a golden retriever. He spends his spare time supporting Reading FC, watching cricket, gardening, reading and, of course, writing. *Management Starts With You* is his first book.

Other Titles

Coaching Skills for Leaders in the Workplace

Developing Mental Toughness

A Practical Guide to Mentoring

Managing Conflict in the Workplace

Setting Up and Running Effective Staff Appraisals and Feedback Review Meetings

How to be Confident and Assertive at Work

Management Starts With You

Alan Hester

A How To Book

Robinson • London

ROBINSON

First published in Great Britain in 2017 by Robinson

1 3 5 7 9 10 8 6 4 2

Copyright © Alan Hester, 2017

The moral right of the author has been asserted.

A CIP catalogue record for this book
is available from the British Library.

ISBN: 978-1-47213-730-2

Typeset in Times New Roman by TW Type, Cornwall
Printed and bound by CPI Group (UK) Ltd, Croydon, CR0 4YY

Papers used by Robinson are from well-managed forests and other responsible sources.

MIX
Paper from
responsible sources
FSC® C104740

Robinson
An imprint of
Little, Brown Book Group
Carmelite House
50 Victoria Embankment
London EC4Y 0DZ

An Hachette UK Company
www.hachette.co.uk

www.littlebrown.co.uk

Contents

Introduction

There are many definitions of management – here's mine, and with it a big hint as to why I have written this book and what it can do for you and the people who rely on you.

Management is about
Getting things done through other people
by
creating an environment that enables them to give of their best.

In my career I have worked with a large number of managers. I've worked for them and with them; I've trained them and managed them; I've sat in board rooms and team meetings with them; and I've been one myself at every level from first line supervisor to director. None of that gives me the right to judge anyone or claim any kind of infallible knowledge, but it does help me to understand and empathise as they juggle the complexities and challenges of what can be a stressful and demanding job.

We can't all be leaders and managers, nor should we if we would be happier and more useful doing something else. You may try it and decide it's not for you, or turn it down because you want to go in another direction. If so, great: choose your path and enjoy it. Many people, however – too many, I think – enter management or progress into senior leadership positions and genuinely suffer. They worry, stress and come to see themselves as bad managers and even as inadequate people because they allow themselves to be ground down by their responsibilities, by those they are supposed to be managing, or by the people who are meant to be managing and supporting them. They carry these feelings with them, and allow them to leak into their family and social lives, and even run the risk of making themselves genuinely ill. This book is for them, or for people at risk of allowing that to happen.

If you are a leader or manager with responsibility for getting things done through others, this book will, I hope, help you to turn these negatives into positives. Management can be, and must become if it is to be done successfully, a powerful and empowering role that contributes to the success of your organisation. It should also be personally rewarding, leaving you with the feeling that you are learning, achieving and taking your people with you. So how do we achieve this?

This book will take you through a journey – your journey and mine, and that of anyone who wants to be the best leader or manager they can be. There will be tools and techniques to help you through specific situations and tasks, but there are a lot of places you can go to get these. You have chosen a book that will help you with the most important part of the job: *you*. Even the best tools and techniques, no matter how useful, will really only help if you are in the right place, personally and professionally, to use them. The best managers know how to manage themselves effectively, because until we can achieve this, we can't possibly hope to manage others. In order to achieve this, we must be prepared to do some real work on ourselves, honestly and consistently, in order to be the best we can be. Only then can we reasonably expect our staff to give of their best.

I often say to managers that their teams resemble them. A scary thought maybe, but a powerful one: you are the role model for your team or organisation. If good leaders make good followers, what kind of followers would a great leader make? Let's find out.

1

All About You

*My first management position came in my mid-twenties when my
then boss announced that I was being put in charge of three offices
and thirty staff in three different towns. I remember walking into an
office where everyone was busily chatting away and then suddenly
went quiet as I strolled the length of the building to my little office
at the end.*

Most of them were older than me and knew more about the business
than I did, and one or two of them (possibly correctly) thought they
should be in my shoes. I had no training, at least not until a year and
a half later when I was sent on a company-wide course for 'new'
managers. Now I know there's no substitute for the University of
Life, but 'sink-or-swim' is not a great approach to preparing people
for high office.

I survived (just) and eventually thrived; I managed in a variety
of organisations until I became a training director with a £12m
budget and then deliberately took up the challenge of becoming
an operations director, with a budget one tenth of the size but way
more real responsibility.

I learned all the time, and I'm still learning now. I learnt from that
first promotion and from sitting in a newly polished office some

fifteen years later with a fancy title and an entire organisation waiting for me to do great things. George Bernard Shaw said that experience is the name old people give to their mistakes and, as we all do, I've learnt from experience. I've also learnt from running a team that became the best in the country at what it did.

What if they don't like me?

For most of us, our first experience of leadership comes as a result of internal promotion. In other words, someone, usually our own manager, recognises our potential and offers us the chance to supervise others. This means that we must have impressed them with our attitude to work and our ability to achieve, as companies will promote only those who they feel will do a good job for them.

So, why do so many young or new managers find their first management role so difficult? By the way, this also applies to much more experienced managers, a significant number of whom have spoken to me about 'Imposter Syndrome', where they describe sitting in their office behind a door with a name plate and fancy title, with the fate of an entire organisation resting on them, all the while wondering to themselves: 'Do they have any idea who they've put in charge here? It's *only* me!' In fact it happens to most people with an ounce of humility in them and I think, as long as it doesn't paralyse you completely, it's a good thing to think in small doses and shows that you are aware of the responsibility you have taken on.

When the office went quiet as I walked in, I assumed they must have been talking about me. How's that for an ego? But I was almost certainly right. I also assumed that they weren't saying anything nice. I was probably right about that too. Did it matter?

At the time it mattered quite a lot. New in the role, I hadn't been trained, coached or supported in any significant way and, let's face it, I wanted to be liked. So it felt like a big deal, and I worried about it and duly felt uncomfortable enough to try to make them like me. Naturally, this didn't work, because you can't make people like you.

This was my first real lesson in management: some people won't like you. It may be because they want your job, or it could be because you're not a very good manager yet. Or it might just be that this is the natural order of things, and part of your role as a manager is to get talked about, criticised or even made fun of. Can you honestly say that you haven't done it yourself? Or still do it today? Thought so! Still, no one likes to be talked about or judged in a negative way so how should we react?

The lesson I took from this experience (painful at first, as so many ultimately correct responses are) was that, while it is always more pleasant to be liked than disliked, being liked is in itself irrelevant to effective management. What you need as a manager is respect rather than popularity. Clearly, respect has to be earned rather than expected, but the behaviours that bring you respect are very different from those that you may be tempted to use if you are simply seeking to be popular. Seek popularity and you may be inclined to ingratiate yourself with people, leading to unhelpful behaviours such as acceding to unreasonable requests, bending the rules or offering something in return for nothing. These will unfortunately not make you popular but instead ensure that you are seen as weak. Appeasement never works! Respect is more of a slow burner; it's earned by qualities such as consistency, fairness and integrity – none of which guarantee popularity but all of which are essential to eventually earning the respect of others.

There is an iron law in operation here, and it's this: the minute you stop worrying about something, it stops being important and in turn stops affecting you. On the other hand, the more you obsess about something, the more important it becomes until it dominates your thinking so much that you cause the very thing you are trying to avoid. But let me explain this process a little more.

Worrying about being unpopular makes you hypersensitive to any perceived slight, so you start looking for problems where there aren't any or exaggerating any difficulties that are really there. Because you believe something is true, you look for evidence to support your belief. Sure enough, if you go looking for it then you will find it and when you do, it will affect you even more. All of this damages your self-esteem and therefore undermines your confidence, leading to more feelings of insecurity and more unhelpful behaviour on your part. This is how people can sabotage themselves and bring about the very things they are so keen to avoid. In other areas of life this is the reason why, for example, a person who is afraid of loneliness often ends up being lonely or someone who is constantly worrying about money never has enough of it.

The only answer to the fear (or reality!) of unpopularity with staff or other colleagues is to accept it as a natural stage in your development and theirs too. As the relationship between you builds, they will see you for what you actually are and not what they have prejudged you to be. For me the turning point all those years ago was when I decided that if someone was going to talk about me anyway, I would prefer them to do so because I was doing what I thought was right, and not because I was trying to please them. Ironically, but totally in accordance with the 'iron law' described above, the moment I stopped worrying about what they thought everything improved. There will always be someone who isn't your biggest fan, but so long as you are doing what you know is right then the solution to that is simple – tough!

> ***No one can make you feel inferior without your consent***
>
> Eleanor Roosevelt

How do I make them take me seriously?

The short answer to that is when you take *yourself* seriously. Until you do, why should anyone else? To clarify, I don't mean taking yourself seriously in a po-faced, standing-on-your-own-dignity kind of way; it's more a case of believing that you are entitled to be a manager and are therefore entitled to manage. Also, you can't make anyone do anything. If you don't like the reaction you're getting from other people, change your own behaviour. This gives them something different to respond to and will affect the way they react. The way you communicate leads directly to the way that people respond. If you are hesitant and obviously lacking in confidence it is difficult for people to trust in your decision-making, but if you are clear and calm when speaking, you will be much more credible.

Clearly confidence is a major issue in the workplace, and not only for managers. One of the key themes of this book is the human need for security and safety as a prerequisite for taking the risks necessary for progress and development in organisations, and if we are lacking in confidence then we are going to feel less secure. This applies to team members, supervisors, managers and leaders. In the next chapter we will look in more detail at some approaches to building our self-belief as a manager, and in later chapters we will explore this issue further by considering the manager's role in creating the culture of trust and security essential to high-performing teams. In other words, we will be working on the second part of my earlier definition of the manager's role: creating an environment in which people can give of their best.

I would like to make an obvious but important point at this early stage in the journey we are taking. Moments of insecurity, indecision or crises of self-esteem are not the sole preserve of new managers. Earlier in this chapter I mentioned Imposter Syndrome, in which the most senior leaders, with a lifetime of achievement behind them, can suddenly question their own ability to make a difference to their organisations. Senior managers are by no means immune to self-doubt. They can lose their nerve before an important meeting, wonder how they can carry colleagues with them on a controversial change, or become frustrated when the managers and teams reporting to them don't seem to take them or their instructions seriously. Managers, team members and chief executives, we are all human, which means we are complicated and often conflicted creatures. It also means we are capable of sustained brilliance if we handle ourselves effectively and relate well to others.

I want to enjoy my job

We will discuss motivation later in the book when we look at creating and maintaining a secure and effective team that gets results. As a vital first step, of course, we need to be motivated ourselves, and while it would be nice if we could guarantee that our own line manager would help us with that, we have to work on the assumption that there is really only one person who can take control of our own motivation.

Control is an appropriate word here, although it's one that some managers shy away from, thinking that they should at all times be democratic and inclusive. We absolutely do not want to become dictators (although sometimes, of course, we will need to be) but equally we cannot afford to be indecisive and allow ourselves to become sidetracked from what we know we should be doing. The best way to gain control over something is to have a clear focus on the result we are working towards and the actions we need to take in order to get there.

Research into what motivates us shows that it is all about achieving things and feeling that we have made a difference. In other walks of life it is much easier to see what we have achieved: a builder can see the house rising from the foundations and know that the wall is higher today than it was yesterday, whereas a manager could work hard all day and find that they have, apparently, achieved nothing. All we have are the goals that we have agreed for ourselves and our team, and the knowledge of how much progress we have made towards achieving them. If we know we are making progress then we feel motivated; if we don't know what progress we are making, then motivating ourselves to keep on trying is difficult.

No one likes to keep banging their head against a brick wall; we all like to see that we are getting somewhere. In the next chapter we will look at some simple but oft-neglected things we can do to make sure that we stay focused on our goal and avoid our energy becoming dissipated by doing things that get in the way of our own success.

> *Our life is frittered away by detail ... Simplify, simplify.*
>
> Henry David Thoreau

Work is making me ill – i want to quit!

There are many ways of dealing with difficult situations. The wonderfully named Thomas-Kilmann Conflict Mode Instrument is a questionnaire that identifies your most commonly used strategy for dealing with conflict, listing five conflict-handling styles: Avoiding, Accommodating, Compromising, Competing and Collaborating. All of these styles can be appropriate or inappropriate depending on the situation you are dealing with. As with most models of this kind, however, the thing to look out for is whether you are acting out of fear or choice.

The urge to quit or to avoid an unpleasant or unproductive situation is a natural one: it makes a lot of sense to avoid danger and one of the simplest ways of doing this is to remove yourself from the source of threat, in this case your job. Your brain is quite reasonably saying: the job is making me unhappy and being unhappy is not good for me, therefore I need to leave. This response is rooted in our evolutionary history and is part of our instinctive repertoire of responses to danger, usually described as the fight, flight and freeze response.

Before we do the bidding of our instinctive programming, however, we need to make use of a more recent addition to our armoury. We have evolved the ability to use reason as well as instinct, so we now have the additional option of thinking before we act. This enables us to use what I see as the most powerful tool at our disposal: we have the ability to make reasoned decisions, the power of choice. Therefore we can move beyond the primitive, reptilian part of our brain that is capable only of responding to immediate events with instant emotions. Instead we can take a step back and gain some perspective instead of going straight for the knee-jerk decision.

It may be, after thinking everything through, that leaving is the best alternative, but before deciding that we can only benefit from applying the reasoning part of our brain. In his book *The Chimp Paradox*, the psychologist Professor Steve Peters describes the human brain as consisting of three separate entities. The primitive brain is our inner chimp and is responsible for our selfish, emotional or defensive behaviours. This part of the brain is the quickest to react and the most powerful, being six times stronger than the human brain, which is the one that is capable of reasoning and analysis. Our success as an individual depends on the ability of the human to 'manage' the chimp, which it does through reassurance, clear thinking and, above all, dealing with facts rather than emotion. The third part of the brain is the computer, which stores and faithfully reproduces whatever information is given it by either the chimp or the human. The computer then creates a 'world view' or paradigm, an established pattern that in effect programmes our response to any given situation.

If the urge to leave – to escape from danger – is the result of the chimp sensing plots and calumny everywhere then it may not be the decision that is best for you. If it's the result of the human making a rational decision that your abilities would be better employed elsewhere doing something more worthwhile for you, then to leave might well be the best decision. By the time you finish reading this book you will know whether it is the chimp or the human talking.

Our subconscious mind is incredibly powerful, but it can and does get things wrong. As Professor Peters argues, the chimp is stronger than the human so we have to be on our guard if we want to ensure that our decisions and actions are the result of rational thinking and not arising from emotional states such as paranoia, frustration or the most common culprit and the daddy of them all: fear. We are programmed to seek pleasure and avoid pain, so quitting a seemingly impossible position seems the most sensible course of action. So what's the problem with that?

The problem may be that we are attaching the emotions of pleasure and pain to the wrong things. Consider someone who goes on a diet in order to lose weight. How many people do you know who spend all day talking about the food they are *not* eating while rewarding themselves with a food-related treat later in the day? They know they shouldn't but they can't help it and justify themselves by saying that they 'deserve' it for being so good, or 'it's only one and I didn't eat anything bad yesterday'. Can you spot the issue here? Fattening food is a 'treat' and a 'reward' so what is the dieter's brain going to be thinking about all day long? Dieting is hard so every day they are 'on a diet' is a day spent going through the pain of controlling their natural urges and denying themselves pleasure. It's no wonder that the clever subconscious is going to argue the case for a treat and come up with all kinds of reasons why dieting is pointless and won't work. The same process is what makes a smoker smoke themselves to death despite being fully aware of the risks they are taking with their health.

A lifestyle change will only be sustained if pleasure is associated with something of greater value to the individual than their previous unhealthy behaviour. They need a good enough reason to commit to it, maybe being healthy enough to play with their children or staying around long enough to play with their grandchildren. Whatever the reason, once found pleasure is associated with the new behaviour and pain with the old.

What has this got to do with a manager wanting to quit a frustrating job? How would you feel if you allowed 'them' or 'it' to defeat you? And how will you feel when you achieve the things you want to achieve? What would it mean to you to work with others to create something really special and be able to say, together: 'We did it!'? Are the things that are getting in your way now permanent features of your personality, the role, the people you work with or the company you work for, or are they temporary frustrations and problems that you need to overcome in order to achieve your goal? Do you have a clear picture of what that goal is? Is it something you think is worth achieving? The issue is whether you are associating pain and pleasure with the right things. Only you will know that but it will become much clearer as you work your way through the following chapters.

All About You: Takeaways from Chapter One

♦ Some people won't like you, but that's all right

♦ Respect is more valuable than popularity

♦ Stop trying to be popular! The behaviours that earn respect are different from those which we use to court popularity

♦ Worry takes you backwards but thinking takes you forwards

♦ We seek pleasure and avoid pain. Make sure you associate pleasure with the most productive behaviour and pain with the least productive – not the other way round!

♦ Don't give up before you've started.

2

Managing Yourself

In order to successfully manage others, you first need to manage yourself. This applies to every aspect of management, whether emotional (mood, language, attitude) or practical (organisation, knowledge, planning). An indecisive manager can't empower a team to make good decisions any more than a manager who is lacking in confidence can inspire confidence in others.

The previous chapter dealt with some very personal barriers to seeing ourselves as 'worthy' enough to lead others, such as confidence, vulnerability and sensitivity to criticism. Managing yourself may not be easy, but it can and must be learnt in order to become the excellent leader that you want to be, and that your team needs. Here are just a few of the challenges that we need to overcome if we are to manage ourselves effectively:

◆ Our emotions – effective leaders have emotional intelligence (of which more below)

◆ Our time – if we waste our time, we are wasting the time of those who rely on us

◆ Our focus – what we focus on we get more of, so we need to focus on the right things

◆ Our values – consistent values mean consistent behaviour and decision-making

◆ Our belief – setbacks are inevitable on the road to success, so use them to strengthen resolve rather than weakening it

◆ Our attitude – people need their leaders to be positive, so be someone they want to come to with their ideas, mistakes or problems, knowing you will work with them towards a solution.

Managing with emotional intelligence

This chapter is about the process of managing yourself. Our challenge is to be 'emotionally intelligent', recognising and understanding our emotional responses well enough to allow us to control them, instead of being controlled by them.

Emotions are complex and powerful – after all, we've spent years being ruled by them and interpreting everything through them. Like a lot of other things in our lives, our emotions quickly become habits, and the longer we react in a particular way the more ingrained those habits become. There's nothing wrong with feeling strong emotions; they can drive us on to achieve against the odds or help us to empathise with others. However, they can also cause us to overreact in situations where a clear head would serve us much better.

Managing ourselves means that we learn to think before we react. The emotional responses of fight, flight or freeze are instinctive reactions to perceived danger and, while they made a lot of sense when humans lived in a wilder state, they are of limited use in the modern workplace. When people are looking to us to work with them to fix things or come up with positive solutions, they are not really looking to us to punch someone, run away or dither; they are looking for someone to act responsibly, decisively and calmly.

We are not machines, and I am not recommending that we try to become emotionless in any way – we need our emotions to help us relate to people, communicate authentically and share in common experiences. An emotionally intelligent manager, however, recognises both the feelings engendered by a given situation and the habitual response those feelings produce. They are then able to take a step back and assess whether or not that instinctive response will produce the right results.

Ask what you most want and need from a good manager and you are likely to come up with some of the following: someone who is consistent, calm and approachable and who listens to what you have to say with genuine interest. You will respond more positively to a manager who shares information with you and invites questions rather than one who keeps things to themselves. Other important attributes of an ideal leader may include giving credit where it's due (ideally in front of other people), or a leader who is slow to blame others for mistakes and quick to help them to learn and develop.

This 'paragon' of virtue is, quite simply, a manager with sufficient emotional intelligence to separate their own concerns from the needs of their team, their task and the individuals concerned. The above characteristics are all those of a manager who is comfortable enough in their own skin to be able to respond to a situation on its merits and not as a result of any preconceived ideas or personal agendas.

I want to be more confident and more decisive. Where should I start?

What is it that enables someone to think and behave as the 'ideal' manager described above? And why can it seem so hard to do it? How can we develop the confidence to deal with everything professionally and calmly, and not overreact or panic so much that we get thrown off course?

Confidence, and along with it assertiveness and clarity, is not a natural behaviour for most of us, so if you struggle to remain in control of everything you are not unusual. However, without confidence managing others will be an uphill struggle so we owe it to ourselves, our team and our organisation to work on ourselves until we can give at least a convincing impression of it!

One important thing to remember is that you were given the role you have as a result of what you have already achieved. What does this mean? It means that you don't need to try to be anyone other than the person you are – there are as many ways to manage as there are managers. If confidence means anything at all, then the first thing it must mean is that you have the confidence to tackle the role in the way that works best for you. If you are a quiet person, pretending to be a loud, brash motivator will not work for you, so don't even try. Be proud of who you are and what you bring to the role. The only requirement of you is to develop the confidence you need to be the best version of yourself that you can be.

Confidence comes from two sources: one is self-esteem and the other is achievement. In other words, what we think of ourselves and what we do. As we saw in Chapter One, the more we value ourselves, the more likely others will be to take us seriously and do what we need them to do. Here, I'm not talking about misplaced self-belief or what is commonly seen as arrogance as that particular type of self-belief can cause people to behave in ways that are unconducive to good management.

Lack of confidence stems from a concern that we may not be able to handle the challenges we are facing. We don't believe enough in our own abilities, perhaps because we judge ourselves to have failed or because others have judged us in the past. This means that when attempting to deal with a situation we carry in our minds the memory of past failures or unfavourable judgements, and we go into this new situation with only negative predictions of the likely outcome. We then lose confidence in our original decision and therefore fail to commit to a course of action, convinced that it won't work, or someone will find fault with it.

The perfectionists among us delay and miss the moment because they are waiting until they have covered every eventuality and are guaranteed perfection or complete success. Whatever the underlying cause, this lack of 'nerve' then has the predictable result and we convince ourselves even more that we are somehow not up to the task.

You are not as important as you think you are

What? Up to now we've been talking about nothing else! Being yourself, managing yourself and working on yourself are all important and unless you are prepared to do plenty of all those things then you will not become the brilliant manager you have the potential to be. There is a big difference, however, between working on something and worrying about something. Worry takes you backwards and gives you more of the problems you are worrying about, because your brain is focusing on what is going wrong instead of what you can do about it. Working on something means thinking about it, and thinking leads to action. There is a world of difference between worrying about something and thinking about something, and we will always do better if we spend our time and energy looking for solutions rather than problems. We will also be of much more use to our team and our organisation.

Remember, your team are not thinking about you, they are thinking about themselves. They are interested in you only to the extent that what you do affects them. That doesn't mean they are selfish or uncaring, it simply means they are human. This is important knowledge because it is easy for us to get so caught up in our own concerns that we forget our job is to help people to deal with theirs. Accept that we are up there to be shot at, but also that this is by virtue of our position. It's not personal (at least to start with!), it just feels that way to you. If people resent you because they wanted the job you've been given then they resent you because of the impact on them – it's their issue, not yours. If they object to a decision you've made, it will be because of the way they think it might affect them.

When recording the original 1984 Band Aid single 'Do They Know It's Christmas?' singer-songwriter Bob Geldof had to deal with a studio crammed full of super-rich, egotistical pop stars, all with their own fans, careers and images to maintain. He pinned a large notice at the entrance saying: 'Leave your egos at the door'. To a large extent we need to take his advice too. So stop worrying about whether other people are looking at you, judging you or talking about you and think instead about doing the best job possible and enjoying working with others to produce something great.

It's not all about you, but it is all about how you do your job. There is a difference.

Work on yourself for better results

Management, like life, is full of apparent contradictions. As we saw in Chapter One, the first step towards earning respect as a manager is to stop trying to be popular. Now we find that the less we worry about our own ego, the better we are likely to feel about ourselves. Confidence is really a by-product of achievement: we feel confident when we succeed and our self-esteem increases when we can see that we are making a difference. The moment we stop focusing on ourselves and our insecurities and focus instead on working with others to find the best solution is the moment we start producing evidence of achievement.

> *A driver is horribly lost on a country road and is getting more and more confused. Finally, he stops next to an old villager, winds down the window and asks: 'How do I get to Bristol?' The old man strokes his chin and thinks for a moment before saying, 'Ah, well. I wouldn't start from here.'*

When it comes to self-development there is only one place and one moment we can start from, and that of course is the here and now. It's also the very best place to start anyway, as it contains all the information we need.

There are some simple things we can do to become more effective and they fall into one of two categories: things we should start doing and things we should stop doing. Of course these will be different for each person reading this book: you will know which behaviours help the achievement of your goals and which ones don't. To help you to understand some of the most common issues and chart a way forward, here is an introduction to some practical tools and techniques, starting with the instructions you are currently giving yourself and which are leading directly to the results you are currently getting.

The power of 'self-talk'

The essence of management is of course communication. Our role involves communicating effectively at all levels, both inside and outside our organisation. Before we can effectively communicate with others, however, we need to pay some attention to another aspect of communication and that is the messages we give ourselves through our self-talk. Why? Because our own internal dialogue plays a central role in deciding the outcome of everything we do.

So, what is self-talk? It's the voice in our heads that provides a commentary on everything we do. Susan Jeffers, in her classic self-help book *Feel the Fear and Do It Anyway*, calls it the 'Internal Chatterbox' and blames it for every missed opportunity and botched decision she ever made. It's the voice that tells us what to expect from any situation and provides an opinion on our own ability or the likely response from the person we are dealing with.

Most people's self-talk is negative, creating an expectation of failure, difficulty or discomfort. Why this is the case is the subject for another book, but most of us are unaware of the impact of these constant messages telling us to aim low, prepare for failure or at least be cautious and hedge our bets. If we are to manage ourselves successfully we must therefore manage our self-talk. This means listening out for what it's telling us, and changing the message.

A manager told me one day how much he hated giving presentations. Every month he had to stand up in front of a meeting of senior managers and directors and present on the past month's performance. He told me that:

- No one is interested in what I have to say

- The senior managers spend all their time tapping on their phones or iPads

- I am a boring presenter anyway

- I hate giving presentations

- I can't see the point in it when they've had all the information already

- I dread every monthly meeting because I will have to go through it all again.

The message he was giving himself was that he was a bad presenter and his audience wasn't interested. If that were really the case, what was the point of giving the presentations? How hard would he work on preparing his next presentation? How would he feel as he delivered it? How good was it likely to be? Naturally it was a self-fulfilling prophecy: what he had done was to talk himself into giving dull presentations. In other words, he had given himself a direct instruction to feel negative and perform badly. What we think leads directly to what we do, and what we do leads directly to the end result.

So, what could he do to break this pattern? The answer is to address the root cause and change his self-talk from negative to positive. Between us, we came up with positive versions of each of his original complaints and produced a list that looked like this:

◆ Everyone is really interested in what I have to say

◆ The senior managers are making notes on all the points I'm
making

◆ I am a great presenter

◆ I love giving presentations

◆ I have the opportunity to add interesting insights to the
information they already have

◆ I look forward to every monthly meeting and the opportunity to
tell the management what my team has achieved.

In fact both sets of statements are lies. His original self-talk is made
up of lies that happen to be negative: he cannot know as a fact that
no one is interested, or that every audience member is writing their
shopping list while he is talking, or that he is boring. The second
set is also lies. In particular the point claiming that he loves giving
presentations – he clearly doesn't!

Up to now, though, he has believed the negative lies and, guess
what? They have become true and set him on a downward spiral of
dread and poor performance, sapping his energy. All he has to do
is believe the second set of lies, the positive ones, and if he gives
himself these messages before his next talk they will also become
true, and something very interesting will start to happen. For our
brains dislike tension and if we give ourselves a positive reality to
prepare for, we will behave in accordance with it. This is not magic
or mystery, it is common sense. We don't make logical decisions
most of the time; we believe something and then look for evidence
to prove we are right.

As I worked with this particular manager he began looking for reasons to support the positive statements instead of the negative and his positive mindset drove his preparation, leading him to vary his presentations, include the audience more, and expect them to be interested and involved. The result was a much better experience for him and his colleagues: he did a much better job because he changed his self-talk.

Transactional analysis for managers

Our behaviour leads directly to the behaviour of others and, while it is not the only thing that influences how others relate to us, it is the one thing over which we potentially have total control.

Transactional analysis (TA) is a model for understanding what happens when we deal or 'transact' with someone else. Understanding what goes on in these conversations, how we behave and what results we get can help us to deal with people more productively. In a team situation, these transactions occur on a daily basis and patterns quickly become established through repetition. This is why we often feel that we are having the same conversation with someone over and over again.

Giving a little thought to how we behave and the patterns we have established with our colleagues helps us to understand why they see us in the way they do. Once we recognise a pattern, and can understand its cause, we can set about replacing it with a more productive one.

Here are some questions to ask when thinking about whether TA might be useful for you. Am I happy with the results I get from dealing with other people? Do I feel comfortable dealing with them? Do I get what I want most of the time? Do people sometimes react to me in ways that shock or surprise me? Do I sometimes come away from a situation feeling that I should have dealt with it differently?

TA suggests that each of us behaves in one of three broad ways described as 'states', as in 'states of mind'. These are the Parent state, the Adult state and the Child state.

Parent – In the Parent state, we behave as a parent might behave towards their child and if we behave in this way it is likely our behaviour will have been subconsciously 'copied' from our own parents or carers. In this way, we repeat patterns of behaviour and even forms of words that our own parents used to us. These repeated patterns are fundamental to what TA is about and psychologists call them 'learned' or 'conditioned' behaviours; the behaviour is copied from examples we have seen before and we are conforming to someone else's idea of what is appropriate rather than reacting to a situation on its own merits.

Parent behaviour can either be critical or nurturing.

TA says that our behaviour leads directly to the behaviour of others. So, if we are in Parent mode, either critical or nurturing, we are inviting the other person to respond as a Child. So, let's look at how a Child behaves in TA.

Child – In the Child state, we behave as a child might behave. Since we have all been children, this behaviour is almost certainly a slightly more grown-up version of how we used to behave as children. Children learn very quickly how to cope in the world of the family or the playground. As a child, we had to learn how to get what we wanted, how to avoid doing things we didn't want to do and how to win approval or stay out of trouble. What did you do? (Here, suggestions might be sulking, crying, making people laugh, avoidance, being cheeky, etc.)

Child behaviour can be either adaptive (doing as you're told – or appearing to do so) or free (playing and not taking responsibility).

Adult – In the Adult state we behave as an adult might behave. In other words, as a rational, calm person would react in any given situation. Adult behaviour deals with the here and now, unlike the other two states, which deal with the past. It does not prejudge people or make assumptions, and is not governed by 'ego'. This means that an Adult is able to look at any situation on its own merits and does not have to defend him- or herself against the other person.

If you behave as an Adult, you are inviting the other person to behave as an Adult. This means that you can have an adult-to-adult discussion. An Adult transaction is based on reality, not assumptions, the present not the past, and on facts, not feelings.

If you are calm and logical, you will be able to listen to the other person and respond to what they are actually saying, not to what you *think* they are saying. When you are both 'in the same place' you will be able to resolve the situation more quickly, more calmly and achieve a positive result. Adults respect each other and find it easier to communicate and to build trust.

As managers it is important that we are congruent and give a consistent message in all our dealings with people. This is why managing ourselves is integral to managing others.

Chapter One described how the brain seeks pleasure and avoids pain and suggested that we should make sure we associate pleasure with productive behaviour and pain with unproductive behaviour. I believe that TA has a similar message for us in relation to reward and motivation.

In managing ourselves, just as in managing others, we need to be sure we are rewarding the right behaviour. As the behaviour we want is best described as Adult, it makes perfect sense to reward it. This principle will inform Chapters Three and Four, when it comes to promoting and rewarding productive behaviour from your team. If we don't want to see people behaving in Parent mode (critical parents make at best annoying colleagues or managers) then we need to be clear about the boundaries and standards we should all be working with – including ourselves. If we don't want to promote dependency (Child) then we should make sure we don't reward it by taking responsibility away from people.

Case Study

The chief executive of a charity employing nineteen people found herself facing the loss of two-thirds of her organisation's income overnight due to a change in government policy. Privately, she was devastated. She had personally worked hard for a decade or more to build the organisation up to where it was, and she believed passionately in the services it provided for young people.

Around her she had a team of highly skilled, committed people, who were equally proud of what they did. Now she could see it all crashing down around her.

The 'Child' in her was angry with the government. It didn't understand what it was doing; it was impersonal, clumsy; stupid. The 'Parent' in her felt sorry for her team; she wanted to look after them and protect them from what was about to happen.

She gave herself some time to think about the best way to deal with this unwanted and upsetting situation. During this time she consulted with her board members. She then drew up alternative plans and projections, all of which showed her that the company would run out of reserves within six months and would therefore have to close within three, once redundancy payments had been made and other contingencies planned for.

Once she had worked through these scenarios, she reflected on all that she and her team had achieved, and the difference they had made. She decided that she did not want to give up. Although she had no real idea about how they could survive, she was determined to try. But the problem remained: what should she tell her staff and how should she tell them? She decided to call a meeting of all the staff in the organisation. How she handled that meeting was key to all that followed.

She decided to tell them straight. Pulling no punches, she told them about the cut in funding and how long the money would last before it ran out. She allowed them time to react

> *as she had, with anger, upset, disappointment and dismay. Then she gave them a choice: did they want to fold the organisation now with a planned and managed exit that gave them the time and money to look for new jobs, or would they prefer to stay and work with her to find a better future for the charity?*
>
> *By the end of that first meeting there were working groups established to look at options, including whether to drop existing products and services, change them or launch new ones. There were the beginnings of debates about whether people would pay for what had previously been free, whether the charity could survive commercially and what it would do to their values. She remembers more excitement and creativity in the room that day than there had ever been, yet the team had just been given the worst news, with no promises and no instant solutions. Why?*

The CEO had allowed herself to work through her emotions and her instinctive 'Parent' and 'Child' responses on her own, or with trusted advisers. She also gave her team the time to come to terms with their feelings in an open and honest environment. All her communication with them, however, was what we would describe in transactional analysis terms as 'Adult'.

Adult behaviour is calm, logical and consistent. Behaviours include listening to others, being honest and dealing with reality as it is, rather than getting angry or pretending everything will be all right – very close to the 'paragon' described earlier, in fact.

Being open with her team, she allowed them to be open in return. By facing up to the situation as it was, she was able to get them very quickly from states of anger and concern to those of reason and action. And, crucially, she gave them a choice. If you want people to react in an adult manner, the best approach is to tell them the truth, listen to what they have to say in response, and then offer them a choice as to their next course of action.

Her team responded with enthusiasm and determination, and a lot of creativity, because she had created an environment that enabled them to respond in that way. In other words, she behaved as an adult. This is inspirational leadership, and it is based not on ego or grand gestures and motivational speeches, but firm foundations. Another way of describing her behaviour would be to say she was thoroughly professional. It was the result of self-discipline, honesty and a genuine desire to reach the best outcome from a tough situation.

The CEO wasn't thinking of herself, she was thinking of her team, the organisation and the customer. When you are confident, honest and well prepared, other people can relax and perform better. So can you.

Your team resembles you – so let's make sure it's a flattering comparison!

Managing Yourself: Takeaways from Chapter Two

♦ Before we can manage others we first need to manage ourselves

♦ Managing ourselves means managing our emotions

♦ Don't try to be someone else; you don't need to. You were given the role you have because of what you have already achieved

♦ You are not as important as you think you are! And that's a good thing as being self-conscious is unhelpful

♦ Your team are not thinking about you, they are thinking about themselves. They are interested in what you do only to the extent that it affects them. It's not personal

♦ Draw up a list of things you should stop doing and others you should start doing. The sole criteria will be whatever helps you to achieve your goals

♦ Your self-talk determines the outcome, so keep it positive!

3

Managing Others

Who are you, and what do you want with me?

It's easy to forget where we came from, isn't it? Most managers gain their first management position following promotion from within their organisation and this brings its own threats and advantages. One great advantage should be that we know how the team is thinking because we have been thinking the same way too.

What your team want is likely to be the same as you want, and what they need is likely to be the same too. Think back to what you needed from your manager and you won't go far wrong, particularly if you think of past managers you admired and those you didn't. With this understanding you will know what your team needs from you and you will have some role models to emulate and avoid.

People and process – the twin pillars

As we have seen, management is a complicated business and I could fill the rest of this book and a few more besides just by running through all the various responsibilities and challenges the average manager may have to deal with. When faced with conflicting demands it is easy to conclude there is no way of getting a proper handle on it all, but I prefer to boil all of this complexity down to a few key principles in the belief that if we get those right, the rest will take their rightful place in the queue.

Here, let's list a few of the skills and behaviours we need to be good – or, preferably, excellent – at in order to be a great manager, and some of the situations we need to be able to manage. In no particular order we can identify: communication, time management, organisation, conflict, discipline, objectives, monitoring, planning, change, projects, difficult people, decision-making, motivation, performance, morale, coaching, delegation, advocacy, presentations, report-writing, recruitment, appraisal and so on. It's quite a list, and that only scratches the surface.

However, all of these points come down to just two aspects of the role: 'the twin pillars' of people and process. If we are good with people, relate to them well and communicate clearly then that's half the battle. But if we neglect to develop, implement and communicate clear and workable processes as well then all our good work will be in vain. So, we can be great with people but cause problems if we are not organised, and we can be the most organised and structured person in the world, but if we can't relate to people we won't be effective.

Everything that follows in this chapter needs to be understood and implemented as a combination of managing people and managing process. You can be flexible, but you can't make it up as you go along. A proactive leader who is on top of things, anticipating and taking action, is easier and more encouraging to follow than a reactive one, who is constantly behind the curve and only dealing with things as they occur.

Good people skills enable you to make good relationships, but the design and monitoring of effective systems and processes enables you to maintain them.

Communication for managers

This is a huge subject. Whenever I have been asked to help an organisation to resolve a problem within a team, the first complaint I hear – whether from management or staff – is invariably about communication. Communication can be too little, too late, too incomplete or too one-sided. Staff will tell me that no one listens to them or no one tells them what's going on, while managers in turn might say that no one comes up with ideas or asks questions even though they give them every opportunity. I will confine myself to a few observations here and encourage you to look at your role in the communication within your team.

When I ask groups of leaders and managers why they communicate with their team they tend to come up with reasons such as to explain something, to make sure something gets done or to give them information. These are all perfectly good reasons to communicate with your team, of course, but they are all what I think of as 'me-to-you' reasons: they are one-way, and one-way communication is not real communication. There is a place for it, but if we simply 'tell' or 'sell' then we are missing the other half of the communication cycle. What we are missing if we only (or mostly) use 'me-to-you' communication is the other person's perspective. Without that, we don't know if they agree with us, understand us or have a better idea than we do. In the absence of any feedback all we can do is assume, and that is never satisfactory.

Once they have got their initial reasons out of the way, the list then expands to include other reasons for communication, such as gaining new information, involving people, asking for their input and building relationships. We all know we need to do these things, but they are sometimes not at the forefront of our minds because of the pressure to get the next thing done. However, communication is only genuine if it is two-way.

Case Study

The chairman of Millwall Football Club spent a match day with a member of staff employed to sell refreshments in a catering kiosk. At the end of the match, the catering assistant showed him a pile of thirty burgers.

'What do you think I'm going to do with these, Mr Chairman?' he asked.

The chairman said he didn't know.

'I'll tell you,' he replied. 'I'm going to throw them in the bin!'

'Why?' he asked.

'Because you're too tight to buy me a fridge ...' Here, he paused for effect, then asked, 'How much is each burger? I'll tell you, it's £5. That's five x thirty, that's £150. How many kiosks are there in the ground, Mr Chairman? I'll tell you, there's ten. That's ten x £150 – £1,500 per match. Twenty-four matches a season, that's thirty-six grand a year. All because you didn't think to buy me a fifty-quid fridge!'

So what do you think the chairman did? It pays to listen to your staff – they might just know what they're talking about!

Listening is the most important part of communication. Author Stephen Covey made it one of his seven habits of highly successful people in the phrase: 'Seek first to understand, then to be understood.' A Cherokee saying warns us to 'Listen, or your tongue will make you deaf'. My science teacher at school told me: 'You have two ears and one mouth, boy. Use them in that proportion!' The 'rule' of listening twice as much as you talk is a pretty good one, I have discovered. An essential part of the process of getting to know and understanding your staff, it gives you the opportunity to involve them, to find out how they think and learn, and to use that knowledge to tailor your communication to them.

When we do say something, however, the imperative is to say it clearly. For all the benefits of being democratic and inclusive, people still need to be led. Knowing that there is someone in charge who is thinking and communicating clearly gives them confidence.

Good fences make good neighbours: the difficulty and importance of boundaries

More than anything else, what we are aiming to do in order to manage people effectively is to create and sustain good working relationships. Ask almost anyone what they expect or hope for in a good relationship and they will talk about the need for trust, openness, honesty and good communication and, of course, they would be right: these are important qualities in any good relationship. Effective working relationships also depend on clear boundaries and expectations, so everyone is clear about what is expected of them and what constitutes acceptable or desirable behaviour.

In many ways, although it may not be very politically correct to say so, there are parallels between bringing up children and managing adults. It is widely accepted that children benefit greatly from knowing where they stand, and the most well-adjusted know exactly where the boundaries are: only when you know where they are can you test them.

In the 1987 film, *The Last Emperor*, there is a scene in which the infant Emperor splashes a servant who is attending him while he bathes. Seeing there is no consequence to this action, he splashes another, before soaking as many as he can. He was always indulged and never challenged, growing up to be the weakest ruler his country ever had and overseeing the eventual dissolution of his empire.

The best time to establish these boundaries is as soon as you can. In 'Mending Wall' the American poet Robert Frost wrote of the benefits of a day spent walking the boundaries between his farm and his neighbour's, while they worked together to repair the fence between them. Having established the boundary, they knew where they stood and could work together in harmony: 'Good fences,' he wrote, 'make good neighbours.'

Case Study
A schoolteacher introduced himself to his new class at the start of the school year. Noticing a boy wearing a Tottenham shirt, he told him he was a West Ham fan and spent a few minutes chatting to him and a few other boys about football. When the bell rang for the start of class and he asked them to open their books at page fifty-four, no one did.

> *The teacher had acted as if he was one of the boys, and in doing so found it hard to become accepted as their teacher. He had failed to establish the boundaries before starting a working relationship and subsequently faced an uphill struggle to change the dynamic he had helped to create.*

People often ask me if they can become someone's manager and still be their friend. They worry about the risks of socialising with them as an equal one moment and perhaps 'telling them off' the next. Also they wonder if that person will take them seriously as a manager, or whether they will resent them for it, or think that the new manager has become 'too big for their boots'.

There is no one simple answer to this question, no hard and fast rule that covers every eventuality, as all situations and the individuals involved are different. Some managers feel uncomfortable socialising with their teams outside of work, while others are more than happy with the idea. As with so many things, it all comes down to personal preference.

A manager told me that his boss was trying to pressurise him into joining his colleagues in the pub after work, telling him that he was isolating himself from the team by going home instead. I believe his boss is wrong. That may be her style, but if it isn't his then he shouldn't be forced into complying. If he is professional at work, listens to his staff, supports them and gives them clear direction then why should he drink with them too? Mind you, he also told me that he sometimes wears earphones at work if he needs to get something done and I felt that was perhaps less appropriate as a working style!

The key to dealing with this question of friendship versus management, or formality versus informality, is to recognise that people working together do so most effectively when they are clear about their respective roles. If you understand your own role, including expectations and limitations, and you understand the roles of your colleagues, then you can work together. If there is confusion, then you can't.

> *Being a manager or a team member does not make us more or less important than each other, it just means we have different roles. The success of the team depends on each of us performing that role to the best of our ability.*

A newly promoted manager will go through an adjustment, as will their former colleagues. Both need to get used to the new relationship. However, the only thing that has changed, and the only thing that needs to change, is their respective roles. They are still the same people and if they got on well before, there is no reason not to continue to do so in the future. In order to keep it that way, however, they must accept the new working relationship and ensure that it works for everyone. Here are a few suggestions if you are in this position (they also work if you are an experienced manager taking over a new team or changing an existing one):

◈ If your previous relationship was based on gossip and negativity then you are unlikely to have been promoted in the first place! But if there are elements of this then you will need to resist the temptation to join in. It may initially unsettle others but they'll soon get used to it

◆ If your previous relationship was friendly and involved social contact outside of work, carry on as before. Don't worry about what people think of you, and don't try to be someone you're not – it won't work and it will only make any uncertainty on the other person's part worse by proving that there really is something to worry about

◆ Don't try to 'please' people too much, just do your job well and expect them to do theirs

◆ Involve the team in discussing some of the challenges and responsibilities of your position. Again, not in a complaining or needy way but in a positive one. If they understand why you are now doing different things, or asking different things of them, they are more likely to accept it and work with you

◆ Remember, they are adjusting too so don't be too quick to take offence if they challenge or question something. Instead, deal with it professionally and only discuss the personal aspect if you feel it is getting in the way of their contribution to the team and the task

◆ Share your ideas with them and ask for their input. Then make the decisions you need to make and communicate them with confidence

◆ Recognise good performance with a simple acknowledgement. Raise any issues you need to raise in the same straightforward way. You're only doing your job, and no one (especially your team) will thank you for not doing it!

Feedback and criticism: establishing and reinforcing standards

Have you ever noticed that the people who tell you to welcome criticism and look on it as feedback are those who are dishing it out themselves? No one really welcomes criticism, though some get used to it and expect it. No, criticism is almost overwhelmingly an unpleasant experience. However, what can easily be forgotten is that it can be almost as unpleasant to give criticism as to receive it.

Managers often say that they worry about giving criticism or 'unwelcome feedback' as one delegate euphemistically described it. But it's an important part of the managerial role as we cannot allow poor performance to continue unchecked, so it's a skill we need to master.

The starting point has to be: why are we doing it? What is the purpose of giving this unwelcome feedback? To which the answer must be: in order to help the individual to recognise there is an issue and to overcome it. For the individual, this is a personal problem, but for the manager it is part of the process of continuous improvement of all the individuals in the team and the performance of the group as a whole.

There is a lot of advice around on this topic, much of it useful. Criticise the behaviour, not the person, we are told; deal in specifics instead of generalisations; provide evidence through example rather than hearsay; take ownership of the criticism you are giving instead of hiding behind other people's opinions. All of this is good advice and following these strictures will get you better results than not following them. But is this enough, or will the experience still be a potentially negative one for both you and your colleague?

Criticism is something that is 'done to' an individual, whereas feedback should be different. Feedback at its most useful should be something that is experienced by the recipient as something that is 'done with' them.

The nearest equivalent would be the role of a coach in sport, where the relationship is between a performer engaged in improving their performance and a coach who can offer practical, expert input to help them achieve their goals. Those goals are agreed between them, as are the steps to take towards achieving them, and everything is a process of action, review and planned improvement. Coaching is, in effect, a continuous feedback loop.

Here is a set of suggested principles for handling what I would prefer to call feedback than criticism or, better still, personal, professional and organisational development:

It's a joint activity. Performance feedback should not be a case of you delivering your verdict on someone else. The feedback sandwich was (and still is) a popular method of delivering bad news: the idea being that we 'sandwich' our criticisms between positive comments in a 'Good – Bad – Good' pattern. The idea is that this softens the blow and ensures balanced feedback, thereby sparing the victim's feelings.

There are two drawbacks to this otherwise eminently sensible approach. First, you could camouflage the negative point so successfully that it doesn't register with the recipient, who might instead focus only on the good stuff. If you've used the sandwich in order to make the exchange more pleasant then you may find that your own focus is similarly 'soft' and the issue doesn't get properly addressed. This only delays the inevitable and makes it much worse when you have to raise it again later. Second, your colleague may be the type of person who is highly sensitive to criticism and takes it to heart. This person may not register the good stuff and instead focus only on the negative, which could leave them thinking they're a failure, or that you don't like them or their performance altogether. They will then, depending on their character, argue with you in order to defend themselves, or become personally upset.

An alternative to the traditional feedback sandwich is to begin with their input, not yours. Ask them how they feel things are going (ask follow-up questions if they don't appear very forthcoming). They may say they are wonderful and everything is going well, or they might tell you that they are having problems. Either way, they have had their say and you can now have yours, safe in the knowledge that you have given them the opportunity to give their input and be part of the process.

Whether or not you agree with them makes no difference as you are free to raise whatever issues you wish and, since you have listened to them, they are now in a position to listen to you. Better still, they don't need to interrupt you as they have already given their perspective. It's a conversation, not a lecture. Some of the most powerful behaviours are counter-intuitive and this is an example as you will find it much easier to control the conversation because you are enabling them to play a full part in it.

Agree standards and work towards them. A Monty Python character explained that he had been punished by an underworld figure for 'breaking the unwritten law'. When asked what the unwritten law was, he said: 'I don't know. It was unwritten, wasn't it?'

We cannot ask someone to meet standards we haven't already communicated. The best results are achieved if we agree between us not only what the standards should be, but also what we should expect from each other on the way to achieving them. Agree, or at least explain, what behaviours, results and resources we are here to deliver and clarify roles and responsibilities along with the structures and processes within which they are to be delivered. You cannot fairly complain about something unless you also have a clear idea of what success looks like.

Identify measurement steps along the way. Before you know that someone is competent and knowledgeable enough to perform a role successfully it is your responsibility as manager to monitor and support them until they are at that level. Making someone else responsible before you know that they are competent is unfair. It is also counterproductive as you will end up spending more time correcting errors and limiting damage than you would have spent in working with them to get it right first time.

A straightforward method for supporting an individual to build competence and confidence is to coach them through a process by breaking it into steps and 'signing off' those steps once both you and they are happy with the outcome. If you are concerned that you don't have the time for this, you can delegate the coaching or mentoring role to a colleague. This also gives you the added benefit of giving the mentor recognition for their contribution through providing them with a fresh and interesting challenge.

Build in review and adjustments as part of a process. A frequent error in performance-managing people is for the manager to start the process and then forget about it until the next performance problem arises. If you are genuinely trying to help someone to contribute to the team effectively then you cannot do it piecemeal, fitting in feedback sessions as and when you have the time. This is your job. To rework a famous phrase, 'If you've started, then you'll finish!'

I strongly recommend regular short catch-up or review sessions with staff, regardless of whether or not there is a specific performance issue to address. These are excellent opportunities to review what you are both working on, acknowledge what is going well or not so well, and to discuss any changes that need to be made.

It is easy to think that because we spend so much time in the vicinity of our team (provided, of course, that we do in this age of remote working) we are communicating with them. There is a world of difference between working *alongside* someone and working *with* them.

Look back only in order to look forwards. Patterns of behaviour can form quickly. It doesn't take long to slip into bad habits. This applies to all of us. In working through an issue with a team member, it takes effort to avoid falling into repetitive behaviour. Once an issue has been dealt with, move on and allow the other person to move on as well. Looking back is useful only in the sense that it helps us to understand where we're starting from, establish the facts, discuss reactions to them, analyse the nature of the problem and the possible reasons for it, draw conclusions and then move on.

The only reason for giving and receiving feedback is to decide what action we need to take to find the next solution, then to implement it together. Look back in order to learn, and then use what you've learnt to help you both to move forward.

Each of these five principles can apply to discussions with staff who are currently effective or ineffective, and don't need to be reserved for feedback on negative performance. People are motivated much more by moving towards something positive than away from something negative. Look back only to gather evidence on which to base a commitment to move forwards. Learn together from mistakes and successes, so you both know what will work for you in future.

Managing others is what your job is. Don't apologise for it but don't think it makes you different either. The role of manager is one of many roles in any organisation: do it well and you enable others to do theirs well. The most motivational feeling of all is to leave a day's work feeling that you have made a difference. As a manager, the best way to capture that feeling just might be helping others to feel that they make a difference too. There are definitely worse ways to make a living!

Managing Others: Takeaways from Chapter Three

♦ Managing others is about managing people and process; you need to do both well

♦ Communication is only communication if it's two-way

♦ Listen or your tongue will make you deaf

♦ Good fences make good neighbours. Clear roles and boundaries make all the difference to how people work together. These need to be agreed and consistently reinforced in order to create more freedom

♦ Feedback is precious so do it well and use it wisely

♦ Look back only in order to look forwards.

4

Managing Teams

'It's a jungle out there!'

The behaviour of people in teams is fascinating. Well, that's one word for it. There have been a lot of studies into how people behave differently as part of a group than when on their own. Often, these studies show that they do things as part of a group that they wouldn't do on their own. These include behaving more unkindly towards others at one extreme or sacrificing their own interests to those of the group at the other.

Groups are also the means by which people identify themselves, through their roles, their seniority or their specialist knowledge. The human ability to cooperate with others in groups to form what we now describe as teams has been an important skill in our survival as a species, and has enabled us to dominate our environment in a way that no other species has been able to do. Why, then, does it often prove to be so difficult to get people working together effectively in the workplace?

To find the answer, we need look no further than our closest animal relative, the chimpanzee. Chimps have been observed establishing complex groups with defined roles and leadership structures. Worryingly for us, they have also been observed not only defending themselves against the threat of rival chimp groups but on one clearly documented occasion plotting and carrying out the murder of their manager!

Humans, and chimps, are driven by one overwhelming need: no, not *that* one; the single most urgent need is for security and safety. Without that reassurance, our focus is on self-preservation instead of where we would like it to be, on cooperation and achievement. All or almost all of our behaviour is geared towards keeping us safe from danger. In the world of work we are still driven by the same motivation, and the key to a successful team is to instil a feeling of safety and belonging. Knowing that other people are not a threat, and that our own 'family' group has our back, is the essential first step towards a functioning team.

Without security we cannot be adventurous, as it is too risky to strike out if we have nowhere safe to return to. The biggest single barrier to achievement is fear, and the biggest fear is failure. Successful teams remove the fear of failure from their thinking and focus instead on moving forwards with collaboration and support. It is our job as the leader of this team to identify and neutralise danger by facing up to it and replacing it with a common culture of learning and achievement in a safe environment.

Security and risk

But the very essence of business and competition is that life is not safe and secure, isn't it? Surely the best organisations succeed in spite of setbacks and challenges, don't they? Yes, they do. The other side of the coin is that as well as security we also need challenges to make life interesting. Humans and, indeed, all creatures, plants and all of life grow stronger and healthier as they adapt to the fresh challenges to their survival that the world throws at them. It's the same with business.

Remember the charity that lost two-thirds of its funding? Why did it not only survive but prosper and become a healthier and more positive organisation than it had been when safely funded by central government? I suggest:

- The challenge of having to earn its own money by selling its services rather than offer them free through grant funding meant it faced severe 'evolutionary' pressure that threatened its very existence

- The leader made no attempt to hide the serious nature of the threat from the group but instead gave them all the information they needed to make an informed decision, enhancing the trust that already existed between the team and its leader

- The combination of severe threat and unity of purpose in dealing with it made the organisation more creative, more capable and more motivated than it was when operating within its comfort zone.

I have spoken to the staff since they successfully met this existential challenge and everyone says they would not go back to the old state of affairs, even though they had previously been happy with it. They all feel pride in what they've achieved, enjoyed the process of meeting the challenge and continue to this day to innovate and look forward.

The need for security therefore should not be characterised as a desire to avoid hardship. People and teams will naturally avoid hardship if they can, but if led well and included in the challenge they are more than capable of achieving previously unimaginable results. They will take risks if those risks are calculated ones with the potential to deliver the desired outcome. They will take part in change initiatives if they are involved and feel included and in control. The most powerful instinct is to protect what we already have, so to motivate us enough to override that instinct the desired future state must be more real and more appealing than the current reality.

Security, growth and performance

As the leader, we are responsible for how our team performs. We create the environment in which they work; we provide the boundaries, set the standards and apply them with fairness and consistency. We create and promote the culture in which our team operates. An environment in which everyone knows their roles, understands the rules and recognises that there are consequences for their actions is a secure one.

However, we know that not all workplaces feel secure to those working in them, and we know that the culture in many organisations does nothing to promote feelings of security. Indeed there are organisational leaders who see leadership very differently, and actively promote an 'edgy' culture. They aim to 'keep people on their toes' by setting them ever-changing targets, creating internal competition and testing them to see how they react. This type of leader associates security with stodginess and would be horrified to hear that they could get better results by helping people to feel safe.

This approach, however, fundamentally misunderstands the relationship between security and performance. I understand the concern that people who feel comfortable with their situation may become so comfortable that they settle for mediocrity, and that a complacent team can become flabby and unambitious. We definitely don't want to create that sort of environment for our team. What we do want is a team culture in which people are confident – there is a world of difference.

Confident people are able to speak up if they think something isn't right. They can contribute ideas if they see a way to improve something. Crucially, they are not afraid to make mistakes. If you can create a culture in which mistakes are seen as an excellent source of information and feedback then people will admit to them, discuss them and work together as a team to find better ways of doing things. If, on the other hand, you view mistakes as something to be embarrassed about and immediately start looking for who or what can be blamed, then that is the environment you will create in your team.

This is emphatically not a culture that permits poor performance. You will find that teams who have enough trust to admit their mistakes and work on them are more self-critical, more honest and more effective than those who hide them. Those teams don't hide behind platitudes, don't protect themselves and don't spend their time pandering to their own or their manager's ego. Instead they end up dealing with facts rather than opinion, testing their assumptions against facts and coming up with good decisions and designing robust processes with which to implement them.

There are plenty of reasons to create an open team culture. Without mistakes people can't challenge themselves and grow. Without failures the team can never address them and move on. Without an honest assessment of performance based on facts the team will never understand what works and what doesn't work. Involving the whole team in this behaviour will cement it into the team culture and give everyone a stake in how it performs. Remember, culture is not what we say, it's what we do. Culture is, quite simply, 'the way we do things around here'.

In response to a client questionnaire conducted by the then Department for Employment in 1988, a major reason for failure among those taking part in a scheme to support self-employment and business start-ups was something of a surprise. Early failure often had little to do with business plans, marketing, lack of money or lack of customers. For many respondents it wasn't even a business issue. The single most important factor was the fear of looking stupid in front of their families and friends.

Think about that for a moment. The very people you would expect to be behind you every step of the way, the people you would imagine confiding in and asking for support, and they are the cause of your loss of nerve. This is another example of people being undermined by negative self-talk. It's also a perfect example of the need for security as a base from which to take the odd leap of faith into the unknown or untried.

Without security you cannot be confident, as failure spells disaster. As the charity's team found when it faced up to the unthinkable, real security comes not from denial but from acceptance. People are very skilled at inventing danger and overreacting to it, and once we sense danger our instinct is to protect ourselves. If our team is not a secure environment then each individual within the team will protect themselves at the expense of the other team members. This may take the form of refusing to cooperate, undermining colleagues (including the manager) or paying lip service rather than engaging properly.

This is the road to unproductive conflict and wasted energy. If people feel insecure and you ask them to look beyond themselves they can't do it. Without a safety net, they cannot see beyond the short term and their own self-protection. However, take away the fear and they stop reacting emotionally and start using their skills and determination in a common cause.

Our job is to help the individual team members to feel they are part of something bigger. We, as managers, weave that safety net ourselves out of the best materials such as shared information, feedback, honesty, clear roles, agreed standards, shared resources, common values and behaviours. Those materials are not necessarily soft, but they need to be strong enough to support everyone.

> *People work best when they have individual responsibility within a collective endeavour.*

Understanding teams

The classic definition of a team is that the people in it are 'working together to achieve a common goal'. If there is a problem with team performance or morale it is likely to be because one or both of these criteria are not being fulfilled. Either the team is not working together, or there is no common goal to work towards. These are two aspects of teamwork that you as manager can give your attention to in a number of very practical ways. Here are some of them:

Are the team members working together effectively? Are individuals clear about their roles and responsibilities? Are they aware of the roles and responsibilities of others in their team? Have you identified and resolved any 'border disputes' or personal agendas? Do you recognise achievement? Is the team properly resourced? Is there a regular forum for people to discuss how things are going, clarify misunderstandings or discuss improvements?

Is the whole team committed to a common goal? Is that goal clear enough? Do we all know what success would look like? Does that goal genuinely drive decision-making? Is the goal seen by everyone as positive? Are you actively monitoring performance in relation to the declared goal? Are you feeding back to the team on progress so they know it still matters? Are we assuming that the goal is still relevant rather than revisiting it and refining it in light of changing circumstances?

As the leader of a team you are the conductor of an orchestra. Each member of the team should have a clear role that enables them to make a defined contribution. However, for most of us, we don't have the luxury of standing on the podium in splendid isolation watching everyone do their thing. Particularly in a smaller organisation we are also likely to need to sometimes pick up an instrument and play it, and it's this dual responsibility that can make it a struggle from time to time.

I still think the conductor analogy is useful, even if you spend a fair amount of time with your sleeves rolled up getting involved. We will need to support our staff practically from time to time, we may even have a regular responsibility for delivery as part of our job role, but we are not judged on our ability to deliver; we still tend to be judged on our ability to manage. We are judged by our senior managers, but also by our team. It is our team that will deliver the results, but it is the team leader who is responsible for those results. Given the choice between getting stuck in and doing the job ourselves, or enabling the team members to do it more effectively themselves, I suggest we go for the latter.

If I find that I am frequently stepping in to make sure something is done then there is an opportunity for me to do more than simply share the load. I can do my job as well – I can work out why the task continually depends on me to step in and 'rescue' my team and come up with ways to increase their effectiveness. I can involve my team in finding out what the problem is, and what the possible solutions are: they probably know already, and if they don't then together we can learn in the process of finding out.

The precise action I take will depend on what I find when I look into the causes of the situation. Here are a few possible causes and some possible solutions:

Possible cause	Possible solutions
Lack of resources	Discuss with senior management; remove or reallocate roles
Lack of skills/knowledge	Coaching, training, shadowing
Mission creep	Reaffirm or reassign purpose and scope of team
Lack of planning	Hold team meeting/working group to revisit plans
Lack of decision-making	Provide leadership
New responsibilities added	Revisit job descriptions (this is often left)
Low motivation	Involve senior staff in 'role refresh' with new responsibilities

Out-of-date processes	Throw out old processes and create new ones together
Habits, routines	Pilot new ideas; feedback; multi-skill; peer-to-peer coaching
Lack of role clarity	Monitoring of processes and results; job descriptions again

Just a simple list of problems and possible solutions can be a great little tool. The key is that we are being proactive in our management of the situation; we are thinking like a manager rather than a team member. If we can identify a barrier to performance and improve it we are making a difference rather than coping with things as they are.

If we involve team members in this process they can make a difference themselves, and also see their manager doing something proactive. It gives them a role in addition to their team function and a stake in the overall activity. Most people welcome the opportunity to be more involved and therefore more influential. Helping them to do that is an important part of our role and benefits us by freeing us from being a more highly paid team member. The alternative is that we continue to spend our time *doing* when we should be spending our time *managing*.

Motivating teams

I've heard people say that you can motivate individuals but you can't motivate a team. I know what they are saying: a team is a collection of individuals, each of whom needs to be motivated separately and personally. But I don't see this distinction: of course we want people to feel motivated to achieve for themselves but this is a workplace, and it is important that they are motivated to play their part in an effective team.

Case Study

A team leader in a care home asked my advice about a member of her team. She was an experienced care worker and good at her job, but she had her 'favourite' tasks and was not interested in doing anything outside of them. For example, she enjoyed doing all the washing and ironing for the clients but would not get involved in buying or preparing the food. She wasn't interested in personal development and just wanted to come in, do her job and go home.

The team leader was relatively new in her role, and was also much younger than the care worker in question. She had repeatedly asked the worker to help out colleagues by doing other tasks, and had written a rota, which the woman had got out of by doing swaps with colleagues who were also younger than her and either easy-going or slightly intimidated.

The team leader had run out of ideas as to how to deal with her, had little support from her own manager (whose contribution was to advise her to 'sort it out herself' or 'raise it in the appraisal meeting'). She wanted to know if she should accept that the woman was not ambitious and leave her alone to do the washing.

This case demonstrates neatly the distinction between individual and team needs. There are three aspects to this example, each with their own set of needs and motivations: the personal, team and organisational aspects.

The Person

For the care worker there's no issue: she doesn't want promotion and doesn't need to be developed, so she can't see a problem in coming to work, doing a good job and going home to her family. That's fair enough, as far as it goes. There is no requirement for everyone to be ambitious and want to be developed, and we all need people who will come in and do a good job with little input from us. But she is not the only person involved in this, or affected by it, is she?

When addressing a performance issue like this, we need to think of the overall impact of her behaviour. It may be fine for her, but what about the rest of the team, and what about the needs of the service and the impact on the client?

The Team

There are only so many jobs involved in a care team, and if one person refuses to be flexible she may be forcing someone else to also keep doing the same job. This could soon get dull for them and take away their flexibility, thereby reducing their job satisfaction.

The other team members soon pick up some messages that we may not want them to: for example, if you refuse to do something you can get away with it; and that there isn't really a team at all, just a collection of individuals. This could become a problem for the team leader, as a precedent has been set for others to follow.

The Organisation
The organisation exists to provide a comprehensive care service for its clients on behalf of their families. In delivering that service it is totally reliant on its care staff. It needs loyal workers who will come in and reliably do their job, and while it grows its own managers it doesn't need everyone to want to progress.

However, what it does need is flexible staff who can cover each other's duties and work together effectively to deliver a complete service. It wanted all staff to be multi-skilled so they were confident that each house had a team that could meet all the requirements of the clients.

My advice to her was that while it was fine for someone to stay at the level they wished to, it was not all right for them to refuse to do anything that was within their job description: they are all part of a team and must contribute to it. If we allow one person to become more important than the team then we risk demotivating the whole team for the benefit of an individual.

What makes an effective team?

The short answer is: an effective manager. Although I have known one or two teams who did a good job *in spite of* their manager, rather than *because of* him or her, they are the exception and it comes at a cost to all parties in terms of stress and conflict. Such teams were in any case set up by a previous leader with all the attributes of an effective team. So, what are these attributes?

If we return to our definition of a successful team, it is one in which people work together to achieve a common goal. Dr Bruce Tuckman, a widely respected educational psychologist, came up with the most widely used model of team development in 1965, and it has stood the test of time. He identified four stages that teams go through as they develop: FORMING, STORMING, NORMING and PERFORMING. Later, he added a fifth stage: ADJOURNING.

A summary of this suggests that teams evolve from a collection of disparate individuals with different agendas (forming) and need to discuss, argue and ask questions about their purpose and make-up (storming) before they are in a position to work together. The third stage (norming) is about agreeing 'how we do things around here' – the standards, values and processes that become in effect the team culture. Once these three stages have been completed, the team is ready to deliver (performing). The fifth stage (adjourning) is about change or completion. Each new member of a team, each completed project or, crucially, the arrival of a new manager, prompts activities such as reflection and review.

Every team goes through these stages. The important thing is how effectively they are led through each stage. It is important that each stage is successfully completed. For example, if the Storming stage is badly handled, we could end up with a team in which either:

◆ There are issues that have not been properly discussed.

◆ The loudest or most aggressive person gets his or her way at the expense of everyone else.

Norming will happen whether officially or unofficially. Going to the pub for two hours every day at lunchtime is a 'norm'. Not cleaning customer areas is a 'norm' but neither of these is helpful. The important thing is that the norms we establish create a positive culture that helps the team to achieve its objectives and makes the team a great environment to work in. Remember, a manager achieves targets through the team. This means creating a team that passes the test as a group of people 'working together to achieve a common goal'.

The leader has an important role in team development, providing DIRECTION, SUPPORT and INFORMATION:

Stage 1: **Forming.** People at this stage are still a group of individuals rather than a team and need to be bonded into a team and encouraged to work together.

Stage 2: **Storming.** Team members are getting to know each other and adjusting from being an individual with their own agenda to being part of a new team. This stage can be quite difficult and needs positive handling from the team leader until the adjustment is complete.

Stage 3: **Norming.** The team is beginning to settle down and understand how best to achieve together. It is important to identify clear roles and any gaps in knowledge that need to be addressed.

Stage 4: **Performing.** A strong monitoring process should be in place so that any difference between what *is* achieved and what *should be* achieved can be identified. Action plans to constantly improve performance should be produced and monitored.

Stage 5: **Adjourning.** At this stage it is important to celebrate success and evaluate performance. It is valuable to learn as individuals and as an organisation.

If a new member joins the team, including a new manager, it is important to briefly revisit all stages to take account of the new situation. This avoids 'tired' decisions and missed opportunities for change and improvement. If you are the new manager, then it is worth revisiting all the previous stages with your team. This involves them, informs you and sets the new relationship on a strong footing.

Some thoughts to manage teams by

◈ You create the culture of your team. If the culture you find when you join is not the one you want, it's up to you to change it

◈ In a bad team culture, the people who leave are the good ones. In a good team culture, it's the bad ones who leave. If you build it, they will come!

Managing Teams: Takeaways from Chapter Four

♦ Group behaviour is governed by the need for security and fitting in with team behaviour. This means someone is in charge and taking responsibility for the team

♦ Without security, we cannot be adventurous. Without a plan, we cannot innovate

♦ Security comes from structure, confidence and cohesion. It is our job to provide these through being a role model and creating an environment in which the team can perform with confidence

♦ People work best when they have clear individual responsibility within a collective endeavour

♦ Individuals are an essential part of the team but cannot be allowed to undermine the team ethic by being allowed to behave as if they are more important than the team itself

♦ You as manager create the culture of your team. If the culture you find is not the one you want, it's up to you to change it

♦ In a bad team the people who leave are the good ones; in a good team it's the bad ones who leave.

5

Focus and the Art of Thinking (and Achieving) Big

One morning I was leading one of our regular team meetings when I produced a sheet of paper that sparked twelve of the most fascinating and rewarding months any of us have ever had in our working lives. As the author of a book on management I would love to tell you that it was a stunningly original and inspirational plan I'd spent all night writing up in some frenzied burst of creative inspiration. It wasn't – it was much better than that ...

Our team was responsible for managing the training delivery for apprenticeships for young people in Oxfordshire as the training team for Heart of England Training & Enterprise Council (TEC), the British government's vehicle for managing publicly funded training in the 1990s. The piece of paper contained the results of the national league table of eighty-two TECs across England. I told my team that it showed us as number forty-three in the country. The team's reaction, and mine, to that news has stayed with me ever since, providing a blueprint for future successes and, ultimately, the impetus for this book.

The first reaction was very human: the league table was unfair, it was a stupid idea and why would we be interested in something as coarse and manipulative as that? What was the point of it anyway? Clearly the TECs in the north of England had an advantage ... Cheshire TEC were the government's blue-eyed boys and always won everything ... and anyway, it's only one measure among many and doesn't reflect all the different issues in each area.

I equate a lot of things to football so my contribution was to say that in a four-division league this made us a Third Division team. I added that I wasn't happy about that and asked my team if they were OK with it. Among further disparaging comments about the crudeness of league tables someone suggested that it might be good to make it into the top half, so we were maybe higher up in Division Two. Quickly that became Division One. Then, it happened. One of us, and I still can't remember who, said 'Why don't we win it?'

The knee-jerk reaction was: 'What? Be the best in the country? We'll never do that! There's too big a gap to make up. We haven't got the resources. It'll be a lot of work. No one will support us to do it. It'll take too long.'

Having thought about our own reaction we then looked at the providers (the organisations we contracted the provision to and who actually *did* the training delivery). Again there were barriers: 'They'll never join in with that! They're too cynical. They won't believe us. You can't change them, they're too set in their ways, and anyway they wouldn't be interested.'

Fascinatingly, the more reasons we came up with to reject the idea, the more energised we became. I asked everyone if they were all agreed that we would be the best team in the country (at last, a bit of 'real' leadership!) and everyone said yes. Finally, I asked each team member to come to the next meeting with their thoughts on what needed to happen to make the dream a reality and closed the session. So, within minutes of rejecting the league table as rubbish, saying why we couldn't reach the top, and why our partner organisations wouldn't cooperate, we'd decided to do it.

The next step was … to decide the next step.

The most powerful aspect of this story is the way that we were able to create, build and sustain our momentum. We will go through some of the ways in which we did that in a moment but first I would like to focus on what I see as the main reason that we went on to have such a positive experience as we took this project forward.

Making a commitment

The reason that we were able to work so effectively towards this goal is simple: because we decided to. It really was as simple as that – we made a choice and committed to it totally. Once you've done that, everything is easy. Even the hard work – especially the hard work.

Not everyone can follow the great but somewhat hackneyed advice to find something you love and spend all your life doing it, mainly because often we are unable to decide what that one great passion is and because of that we can't commit to it. It becomes a vicious circle in which we can't commit because we haven't committed; a version of the twisted logic of the old refrain 'We're 'ere because we're 'ere, because we're 'ere because we're 'ere.'

At work, however, we are here because we're here, because we need to earn money and we find ourselves in a job, which, in most cases, would never have entered our head as a possibility when we sat in front of a careers adviser at school. As you're reading this book, you've probably added management responsibilities to that job, so that other people are now depending on you doing it as well as you can. It therefore makes even more sense that the keys to enjoyment of our jobs are to be found in finding a sense of purpose and getting passionate enough about it to make it happen.

A great leader in the workplace is always going to be someone who finds a common cause, commits to it, and works together with a team to achieve it. This may sound obvious but I can assure you it is rare. Why? It's rare because most workplaces seem to be specifically designed to prevent that from happening. At any moment, in many organisations, the declared goal or purpose of the enterprise is not the most important thing in anyone's minds. It does not:

◆ drive decision-making
◆ determine the allocation of resources
◆ get measured or talked about
◆ become the focus of agendas for meetings
◆ dominate planning
◆ determine rewards and recognition.

If the organisation's goal doesn't affect all these things then, when all the glossy brochures and websites are stripped away, in reality it isn't the goal. A goal is something we work towards, talk about, make our decisions on, plan for, measure and judge ourselves on. It is not something we mention from time to time and blame people for when we realise we've missed it.

It's also easy to mistake the often dreaded, frequently non-motivational and usually top-down measurements known as Key Performance Indicators (KPIs) for the managerial equivalent of working to a common goal or set of objectives. They are, of course, a useful and often indispensable tool for measuring performance, but from the point of view of the team or the manager they don't tend to be seen as an enjoyable one. Often they are backward-looking, usually imposed and seen by many as a threat. As one senior manager on a recent training session on quality management said: 'Don't you dare mention KPIs to me – I hate them, it's all we ever hear about!' The essence of her hatred of KPIs was that there was no reward for achieving them beyond having an even more onerous target imposed on her and her team the following year. She saw them as a way of forcing her to achieve more with less and felt that they were simply a method of judging her and forcing her to judge her team on the same basis. Her frustration is understandable, as many organisations operate in this way across all sectors from local and national government to commercial enterprises or grant-funded community projects.

Key Performance Indicators (sorry, Emily!*) are an entirely sensible management tool, but they are only one tool and they achieve nothing if they are not part of a whole process that involves everyone. Top-down enforcement is not the same as top-down commitment. To have a genuine commitment to quality, to an organisational or a team goal, or to a planned programme of work then you must have commitment from as high up in the chain as possible. This emphatically does not mean that senior management issues a decree then sits back and piles on the pressure to those under them to deliver on the 'vision'. What

* Name has been changed.

it does mean is that everyone involved in delivering the vision understands it, understands why and understands their role in achieving it. Senior-level commitment means the same as it does at any level of management: providing direction, working together with a single purpose and giving the necessary support and encouragement. KPIs, or whatever you agree to call them, then become part of the process of working together, helping to keep everyone focused on the desired goal, providing early indications of progress and early warning of problems or opportunities for improvement.

Working together

Having made our commitment to be the best in the country at what we did (or play the league table-making, top-down judging KPI-setters at their own game – whichever you prefer), we then set about doing it.

Here's another thing that is worth acknowledging: the moment we committed was the moment we started taking action. There was no gap between the two stages. We didn't end our meeting with a promise to think about it and return to it later. We didn't congratulate ourselves before we'd actually done anything. We didn't allow any time for the day-to-day pressures or conflicting priorities of the job to replace the priority we had just agreed. In short, we didn't give ourselves time to get back to our normal way of working, dealing with in-trays and queries or even making cups of coffee while we put off getting started on our to-do lists. We went from commitment to action. More correctly, we went from commitment to thinking, which is the precursor to planning, which in turn is the precursor to doing something.

It's a fact that the only way to achieve something is to take action. The American positive thinking writer Jack Canfield breaks down the word 'satisfaction' into its Latin roots: 'satis', which means 'enough', 'facere' ('make') and 'action', so 'satisfaction' literally means, 'to make enough action'. He also argues that nothing can be made without first being imagined or thought of. So in order to achieve something we need to first imagine it (vision), then think about how to do it (plan) and finally do it. And keep on doing it.

In the absence of action, we make room for inaction. Without forward momentum, we stall. If you leave a gap between commitment and action it will be filled with stuff – excuses, doubts, reasons (there are always reasons not to do something) that get in the way and actively prevent us from moving forward. I believe any period at all of waiting around after that initial decision to commit to our goal would have scuppered the whole idea – there is always something more pressing to do than what we really want to do.

My team immediately set about backing up our words with deeds. Our first question was: 'What do we need to do next?' The answer to this question will differ between projects, industries and situations but as an initial question it's a good place to start and the answers you arrive at will start the planning process for you. We quickly identified the following:

- Check and 'clean' the data so we can all trust what it's telling us
- Set up three or four key reports so we can monitor and measure progress
- Inform internal colleagues of what we're doing and get them onside
- Communicate and consult with delivery partners.

This exercise didn't take long. The next step was to agree who would do what. Again, that didn't take long either. And again, I can't look back on the meeting and remember which of us was responsible for each decision, and I'm glad about that as it meant that we were genuinely behaving as a team. The standard definition of a team is 'A group of people working together to achieve a common goal' and that is exactly what we were doing. All I had to do was ask a few questions and confirm each decision as we made it.

It may seem a counter-intuitive statement but when things are working well, it's easy to do the most difficult things. Athletes are familiar with the concept of being 'in the zone' when they are performing at their very best. They talk about having more time than they normally have, seeing things clearly and being able to instinctively make the right decisions. Our meeting was like that; it was easy. Everyone in the room was positive, enthused and contributing to the discussion. Every question had a very good answer and every problem a solution. Instead of leaving with a 'flash-in-the-pan' idea that would never amount to anything, we left with everything a manager and a team could wish for:

- We knew what we were going to do

- We were excited about doing it

- We knew how we were going to do it

- We all had clear roles that matched our abilities and interests

- We had identified resources and agreed them

- We had an action plan with SMART objectives. (The acronym SMART is a well-known tool for setting objectives that are Specific, Measurable, Achievable, Relevant and Time-bound. It is best used as a test against which to judge objectives when first discussing and agreeing them.)

We *knew* we were going to do it!

Purposeful practice

I described the meeting as easy; it was also fun. But weren't we always taught that success is the result of hard work? We're not paid to have fun, are we? What about determination, strength in adversity and self-denial? Also, the manager's responsibility to motivate people? What about putting in long hours of boring work? Nothing that's worth having is easy to achieve, is it?

Am I suggesting that we can get great team spirit, clear direction and winning results without putting in the required amount of hard work? No, of course not. The reality is that this kind of experience – which is the one we are all aiming for – is the result of a lot of time and energy spent in getting as many things right as we can in the first place.

The *Times* journalist and former Commonwealth Games table tennis champion Matthew Syed, in his book on performance psychology, *Bounce*, describes the concept of purposeful practice. This is also behind the idea publicised by author and journalist Malcolm Gladwell and others that consistently high performance, or what he describes as genius, is the result of more than 10,000 hours of practice and improvement. Gladwell cites Microsoft's Bill Gates and The Beatles as evidence for this theory, while Syed argues that at one time in the 1990s no fewer than five of the world's top ten table tennis players came from the same street in Reading, Berkshire. This was due in every case to these performers having the resources and opportunity to practise, in Syed's case being given the key to a purpose-built table tennis practice room near his home as a teenager.

So, what does 'purposeful practice' mean to us as leaders and managers, and is there a meaningful way in which we can benefit from it as a concept or behaviour? I believe there is, and we don't need the key to a special practice area either. The only key we need is to approach the opportunities we already have with the best attitude for us. Every day we have the opportunity to engage in purposeful practice by engaging with our role with the mindset that we want to improve. Everyone does their 10,000 hours simply by coming to work for a few years, but unless we actively make use of that time to learn and improve then we may not get good enough at it to become management 'geniuses'.

So, let's look for opportunities to get things right. Let's put some effort into changing our situation rather than just accepting all of its frustrations and barriers as the way things are. As Mahatma Gandhi is widely quoted as saying, 'We must be the change we wish to see in the world.' I think he meant that if we don't like things as they are, change them.

At this point let's take a reality check. You may be reading this and thinking that the theory is good but I can't change anything here – I'm not senior enough, I don't have the ear of the chief executive and no one would listen to me if I suggested any changes. You may not want to change the world; you may not be in an important enough role or a big enough organisation to change the world. In other words, you may think you have no influence over what happens. I understand that. On one level, the case study I've been quoting about my own team and our quest to be the best in the country could be put forward as an example of what you're thinking. Yes, we were a small team working for an organisation that didn't make too many national headlines for the work it did; the organisation has subsequently been renamed half-a-dozen times and will soon be abolished altogether; and what was the point of achieving what we did if the achievement doesn't change anything in the long run? All good questions; all good reasons for saying why bother?

So, why bother? I'll answer that with a question of my own: Why not? We have one life, we have one career, and we spend an awful lot of time at work. Chapter One describes and sympathises with managers who struggle to make an impact and take on all the stress and disappointment that goes with that. This chapter suggests that there is a better alternative that makes work (and therefore home) a much more rewarding experience.

You are a manager; you are a leader, so manage and lead. You are paid to get things done and you have a team that's paid to get things done, so let's get them done and while we're at it let's get them done as well as we possibly can. Let's give our team the chance to enjoy their work too, and to learn and develop as they do. Our work may not be important on the global stage but I bet it's important to someone; otherwise no one would pay us to do it.

I described our team meeting as easy, fun and productive. That doesn't just happen. When your team achieves it is the result of a lot of hard work, just as an athlete's performance is the result of practice and determination and all the qualities we associate with excellence. Positive things happen in management as a direct result of the work we and our colleagues put in to enable this. Think of the second half of my definition of management: *creating an environment that enables people to give of their best*. Here are just a few of the things that need to be put in place in order to create that environment:

1. Clear direction and purpose for the organisation

2. Understanding of the role of the team in delivering the 'big picture'

3. Clear roles and responsibilities for each staff member

4. Regular and genuinely two-way feedback in the context of clearly understood and agreed standards

5. An opportunity to input ideas and innovation knowing they will be listened to and considered

6. Stretching targets with support and advice to help them to achieve

7. Opportunities to learn and contribute

8. Relevant information delivered in an honest and timely fashion

9. Adequate resources to enable them to do the job

10. Representation and advocacy within the organisation, where appropriate.

These are just some of the behaviours that a team has the right to expect from their leader. Each one contains within it a set of skills and competencies that are needed to enable you to fulfil these roles in a way that will enhance the performance of your team. They also make a real contribution to the feelings of security and belonging your team will have, which we have seen is fundamental to their ability to perform. Time spent on continuously improving these skills and behaviours will pay huge dividends in the results you and your team are capable of achieving. Purposeful practice for a leader or manager means that the hours you spend at work fulfilling your role are not frittered away by doing the many time-honoured things we are all tempted to do but are instead spent on building the skills and behaviours in yourself and your team that deliver the best results.

Purposeful practice may involve reading and research, identifying areas for personal development and working on them, making use of feedback, joining a network of like-minded people, working with a coach or taking the opportunity to stretch yourself with a specific new responsibility. If time is a problem, and it always is, one of the best ways for you to create time is to practise the art of delegation (see also page 92). Used correctly, delegation is also an excellent tool for developing your team and building relationships with team members.

As I argue elsewhere in this book, what I refer to in this chapter as purposeful practice is not simply a solo activity. The key to building effective relationships, planning for success, monitoring and reviewing for continuous improvement and all the other management and leadership activities is not to shut yourself away from your team to make time to do them. It is to work with your team at every opportunity, so that they and you together make these improvements. The goal is to get your team working together effectively, taking responsibility and ultimately building a team of managers.

If your team can work and achieve when you are not there then that is not a sign of weakness or vulnerability on your part, but a sign of strength. The more self-sufficient a team is, the more it will appreciate and trust you. And the more successful your team, the better it reflects on you. If they don't need you to motivate them then it means you have already successfully motivated them through your example and the way you work with them.

A team of leaders

Once you've agreed on a goal that you all feel passionate about, and all believe you are capable of achieving, you are ready to make a plan to achieve it. This may be a detailed written project plan using a range of tools such as Gantt charts (the Gantt chart is a tool for planning and sequencing multiple tasks and deadlines when managing a project) and project management software, or it could be some agreed actions and responsibilities written on a flip chart and typed up later (my preferred method).

In doing so, you have given yourself and your team the single most powerful tool available, provided you use it: focus. It is well known that what we focus on we get more of, so if you focus on all the distractions around you then all you'll get is more distractions to take you away from your goal. If you focus on what you want to achieve, then you will get more opportunities and ideas for action you can take to help you to achieve this. Therefore having a goal, and a plan of how you will achieve it, is the first serious step towards achieving it.

Plans change, so your initial plan is highly unlikely to stay in place unaltered throughout the project. But without a plan, you can't be spontaneous because you can't jump somewhere else without a solid platform to jump from. Our plan was to be number one, which is very clear if also very challenging, so we were unlikely to deviate from that goal. Over the course of a year, however, while we would not want to change our aim we were very likely to need to change the methods by which we aimed to achieve it.

If you have a plan, and it makes perfect sense to have as clear and robust a plan as possible, you have focus. That should make decision-making easy as every decision can be judged on this simple equation:

> *If I do this, will it take me towards my goal? If the answer is yes, then I'll do it. If it's no, then I won't.*

Everything can be judged on this basis. It's simple and powerful and keeps everyone involved and focused on the task at hand. The more you share your thinking with your team, the more they will help you to make these important decisions. Your team meetings should have the goal and analysis of progress at the heart of the agenda. These meetings should be another way of reinforcing the number one priority. This is not restrictive, it is liberating. Irrelevancies can be swept away as you focus only on what is important. Discussions may be long and impassioned, but learn to see them as evidence of how engaged your team is with the core objective. Debates of this nature are wholly positive. You will notice that no one is talking about what they will or won't get out of it personally; they are not challenging the validity or achievability of the goal. What they are debating is how we get there: not if, not why, but *how*. The actions that emerge from these debates will have been challenged, tested and improved upon until what comes out of them will be as good as the team can possibly make it. If the team is properly focused and the debates kept on topic, these meetings will always take you forwards.

The power of clarity

Once we had taken the first set of decisions and got our first results, we invited our partner organisations to a meeting – all twenty-nine of them. I shared with them the results of the national league tables. They chuntered to each other in their groups, made their cynical remarks and said what a waste of time the league tables were. In fact, they said exactly the same stuff as my team had said.

I then told them that we were aiming to be the best in the country within a year. The chuntering was now supplemented by laughter and the shaking of heads. 'No chance' seemed to be the consensus. Again, just like us.

I asked them if they would be prepared to commit to this goal. More muttering and shifting of seats, but this time there was engagement. It was a simple question and it got them thinking – although still largely coming up with reasons why it couldn't be done. What happened as the meeting progressed shows the value of keeping things simple and not getting distracted.

Those of you who have worked in the public or community sectors may well have noticed the 'golden rule' that seems to apply to relationships between service providers and funders. Those receiving the funding resent those who provide it. In our case this was normally shown by a healthy banter between us but it was underpinned by some firmly held beliefs on both 'sides'. Friendly as this was, I think it only served to keep us all comfortable with a status quo in which neither of us had to take responsibility for how things were, and we all had our ready-made excuses for things staying as they were. We rubbed along just fine, but we rubbed along producing third-division results.

The next phase of our provider meeting could be described as a courtship ritual or in business terms as a negotiation in which we used our best negotiating strategies such as 'If you, then I' statements, proposal and counter-proposal and packaging, where nobody commits or concedes to a request until the whole package has been completed. The key to the process was that because we had an interesting challenge that grabbed everyone in our different ways, we were negotiating for the best way of achieving it. Again, very much like our first team meeting. When you're looking for answers rather than excuses it's a completely different situation.

What came out of this was entirely positive. Gone were the old ways of shrugging shoulders and finding reasons why nothing would change. In came real conversations with clarity and honesty. Both sides said things that we wouldn't have said in the old days (i.e. before that day). We cut through the poses and defence mechanisms and challenged each other, and most of us love a challenge.

Here are some of the key gauntlets we threw each other and the agreed actions:

- They told us we were too slow to make decisions, leaving them unable to act quickly
- We told them they 'hid' underperformance from us until it was too late to offer increased funding to those who could make use of it

◆ They told us we didn't give them up-to-date information on changes to funding conditions so they couldn't get ahead of the game

◆ We told them that they didn't attend our information sessions when we put them on

◆ They told us that my team didn't visit them often enough and didn't understand their reality

◆ We told them that we found the visits too predictable and not very informative.

That same day we agreed a number of actions on each side, including:

◆ My team would have the power to make decisions about funding on the spot, with a call to me to confirm what they had decided

◆ Providers agreed to share their results and predictions honestly and openly each month

◆ We agreed a programme of half-day meetings with all providers to share quarterly results and agree actions

◆ We agreed on short monthly meetings between my team and their provider caseload with a commitment to share and make decisions.

Most radically of all, and after much soul-searching between what were to all intents and purposes commercial rivals, providers agreed that we should share their results in a league table of our own and publish it to all members of the delivery network. For them this was a huge leap of faith and was only possible because we were all committed to the end result. This commitment meant that we became a team – we would all be working together to achieve a common goal. We would have to share information, pool resources, trust each other and make decisions based on the facts. In so doing we had to trust the information, trust our processes and believe in the combined benefits of achieving our goal.

Internally we kept the focus by holding quarterly team 'away days' in which team members took responsibility for a specific area of the project, leading sessions on data analysis, performance, methods for improving recruitment or achievement levels on programmes. What did I have to do? Good question. My contribution was to support both teams – my own internal team and the wider one we had created out of our friendly rivals. I gave people my trust and confidence; I gave them credit for their ideas and contributions; I gave them feedback; I kept the faith. I had a team of leaders.

When the results were produced the following year, this team was top. It had become the best in the country at what it did.

Focus and the Art of Thinking (and Achieving) Big: Takeaways from Chapter Five

♦ Commitment is the first step; a genuine commitment to do something means it is likely to get done

♦ Once you've made a choice and committed to it, every subsequent decision is so much clearer than it would be without that commitment

♦ A goal is something we work towards, talk about, base our decision-making on and measure

with these new problems and react to the clamour for immediate action. This is clearly not a good place to be, but it's where many of us find ourselves, day after day. Success, efficiency and even our own health and sanity demand that we sort ourselves out and, if we can, everyone else as well.

Here's another important number: **15 per cent** of our time as a manager is spent looking for things. So you don't believe it? Where's that phone number for the customer who contacted you yesterday, or the file for that client? Which drive did I save that document to that I was working on last week? I know I've got a copy of last year's figures somewhere; can someone help me look for it? If I can't find it, I'll have to put off that meeting I have to go to this morning … I don't know about you, but sometimes I think I'm above average.

Fifteen per cent – almost a day a week out of a five-day working week – is an awful lot of wasted time. It's down to lack of organisation, which in turn is down to lack of planning, which of course in turn is down to a lack of time for planning. You can picture (or remember!) the chaos that quickly ensues as a result of this level of disorganisation and the impact it has on those around us. If we can't control our information or our processes then how can we control anything? Nothing is more calculated to cause panic and confusion than simple everyday disorganisation of this kind. And it's infectious too.

The two-thirds 'rule'

The two-thirds rule affects a certain type of character and again, in a manager, leader or small business owner, this can be costly. As children we tend to fall into one of two character types: those who come home from school on a Friday night and go up to their room in order to get their homework done straight away, safe in the knowledge that they can then spend the weekend doing whatever they want. This child frees him or herself from pressure and avoids having unpleasant tasks 'hanging over them'. The other character type will dump the schoolbag and start enjoying themselves straight away, either by playing or simply relaxing. Come Sunday night or Monday morning however, and they reluctantly pull their crumpled homework sheet from their bag and set about dashing off their homework, often half-heartedly and with no time to check it over.

Character type two will almost certainly have the unpleasant experience of the looming deadline popping into their head at various times throughout the weekend while they're doing something else and have to push the thought away. The Two-thirds Rule is about this character. Either through procrastination, laziness, busyness or disorganisation this rule states that whenever we have a deadline for a piece of work to be completed, we don't even start to work on it until two-thirds of the time has elapsed.

This type of character (OK, me!) might argue, and believe, we do our best work under pressure and may genuinely fit a lot into our working lives. Equally, we may be putting off something we find uncongenial or we might even be a little complacent about our ability to deliver on time. There is one major risk with this approach, however, and it's implicit in Harold Macmillan's observation: things happen. If we leave everything until the last minute, where do we go when something unexpected happens? If we have three days to prepare for an important meeting and something goes wrong on day one, that's not a problem. But if we leave it until day three and something happens that throws us, we're stuffed. Leaving things until the last minute means that we have no contingency time to put things right when disaster strikes, and a minor inconvenience that we can plan a way around becomes terminal and so we go into our meeting unprepared.

I'm too busy to even think!

Everyone I speak to in business these days has the same response when asked how things are going: they all say how busy they are. I say it too. The pace of work is not going to slow down any time soon. This means there are more and more demands on our energy, our stamina and our time.

Traditional time management techniques involve creating space to allow you to work away from the pressures created by other people; they suggest separating ourselves from our colleagues in a variety of insular and often eccentric ways such as holding meetings standing up, giving people strict time slots in meetings or even allowing them to speak only while holding a designated object (like the conch in William Golding's 1954 novel, *Lord of the Flies*). They suggest working at home or putting a 'Do Not Disturb' sign on your door when you have a particularly important report to write.

Now I understand the thinking behind these techniques and sometimes a bit of personal space is important, but I must return to my original point: time management for managers is different from time management for individuals. As a manager we are responsible for creating an environment that enables people to work effectively. This means giving them information, advice, direction, support and, most importantly, giving them our time. It therefore seems to me that telling managers to separate themselves off from their teams is the worst possible advice to give to people who are paid for working effectively with others.

Here, there is a distinction I would like to make about our use of time. There is an old phrase that business owners and managers often use – time is money. Of course it is, but money can be used in many different ways, some sensible and some less so, and it is the same with time. The only difference is that time is a finite resource and once used, it will never come around again. Time, like money, can be spent; it can also be invested. If it is spent it has gone, but if invested well then it gives you a return on your investment. I would like to look at time in this way: are we investing it for a greater return or are we simply frittering it away?

So what is the point of a team in a workplace? It is to get things done in a way that is more effective than if a bunch of people tried to achieve things on their own. What is the point of a manager? It is to steer the ship in the right direction so that the destination is reached in the best possible way. In that context, how much sense does it make for the leader of that team to spend their time avoiding the team members in order to work on their own priorities? I would suggest it makes no sense at all.

If 70 per cent of our time is spent reacting to immediate events in an unplanned way, and if 15 per cent of that time is spent dealing with the consequences of our own lack of organisation, then it is no surprise if we leave important things until the last minute and miss our deadlines when events take us by surprise and we don't have time to change our plans. Then, in order to try to get ourselves back on track, we may be tempted to lock ourselves away from distractions to allow ourselves to focus on the most pressing priorities. In the meantime, while we are struggling to keep our heads above water, what will our team be thinking and doing? 'Time is money' is normally used as a reason to stop talking and start doing, but if that means that we consider cutting down on time spent talking with our staff then it's a false economy.

Working together on the right things

Avoiding our team because they are distracting us from our work is a sign that we are not managing effectively. A team needs its leader to provide direction, drive and support – the things they need to do their jobs effectively. Equally, the leader needs his or her team to do their jobs effectively. There is synergy between the two, and neither will work effectively without the other. Managing the team is your job. If you do it well, they will increasingly be able to manage themselves.

My approach to time management for managers is the exact opposite of putting up barriers to your time and attention; it is to embrace the fact that you need each other in order to be successful. Give them your time and attention; listen and explain, ask questions, involve them in decisions, keep them informed, give them the background to the challenges you are all facing and invite their contribution. Remember, this is not a cost, but an investment.

We cannot escape the demands of other people, especially our team, as it is part of the job. Managing our team is what we are paid for, and we can't manage them by wishing that they would go away. Therefore we must embrace the fact that a lot of our time is going to be spent working with them. What makes this time an investment rather than a cost is the way we spend that time and what we do when we are with them. Dr Stephen Covey, in his seminal work, *The 7 Habits of Highly Effective People: Powerful Lessons in Personal Change*, developed his Time Management Quadrant, in which he divides work activity into four headings:

Box 1 – Urgent and Important

Box 2 – Non-urgent and Important

Box 3 – Urgent but Not Important

Box 4 – Non-urgent and Not Important

Box 1 activities are in effect crisis management, dealing with problems, missed deadlines and other panics in which we drop everything in order to sort out the immediate crisis.

Box 3 can be described as 'other people's priorities'. These are things that are important to others and feel urgent because of the noise they generate. These are the interruptions we all have to deal with, again asking us to drop what we are doing and respond immediately to the needs of someone else, whether by phone, email or in person.

Box 4 is where we go to avoid unpleasant things, to procrastinate or to recover after all the effort involved in dealing with the aforementioned boxes. Making piles of things (rather than filing them properly), making your fifth coffee of the morning or picking something up and putting it down again are all activities people who spend time in this box would be familiar with. Facebook, solitaire and aimless surfing are also giveaways.

Box 2 activities are the most important managerial activities we can do, such as planning, preparation, monitoring, relationship building and research, but they are often put off until some future date because they are not urgent and do not need to be done straight away. However, failure to carry out Box 2 activities is, in effect, a failure to manage. Covey argues that the crises in Box 1 are the result of not doing these important but not urgent things, as most problems are caused by a lack of forward planning or an absence of appropriate systems and processes. We miss deadlines because we didn't plan to achieve them, or monitor the team's activity to ensure we remain on track, or take the trouble to build effective working relationships with those whose cooperation and support we need to help us to meet them. We are easily distracted (Box 3) when we don't have a clear plan or are not fully prepared and focused on what we want to do. We need to retreat from the fray to Box 4 because we are wearing ourselves out by doing all the wrong things. Doing the right things makes everything else easier.

This is an excellent model, from an excellent book. I have taken this one step further in training and coaching leaders by encouraging them to see their team members as an integral part of this process. While Box 2 is clearly the more strategic place for us to be as a manager, surely it is also a place we should invite our team to join us in as often as possible? If we are going to spend 70 per cent of our time with our team, why not spend it in the most productive way possible, by including them in our thinking, building our working relationships with them and involving them in our decision-making?

Here are just a few reasons for including the team in Box 2 activities, rather than excluding them so you can try to fit in some Box 2 time on your own while they flounder around without any input or support from you:

- Targets that people are involved in agreeing are more motivational than those imposed from above

- People work better and are more committed when they understand the reasons behind organisational decisions. Share the big picture with them, including any aspects of it that are still being discussed among senior management

- The more they understand and appreciate what you are trying to achieve, the more they will be able to help you achieve it

- It is the team members who will be delivering the processes through which they will be achieving those targets, so why not involve them in designing the processes? After all, they know the job better than anyone

- Working with you on the challenges facing the team will enhance the feelings of membership and ownership that are essential to team identity and motivation

- The more your colleagues know, the more confident they will become and the more willing they will be to contribute and take on new responsibilities and the less they will depend on you to give them 'permission' to use their initiative

- Individual achievements become team achievements and help to create a positive team culture

- With increased knowledge and shared awareness the team will spend less time asking you questions and more time answering them, reducing time spent in Box 3 for all of you.

The quality of the time you spend with your team improves tenfold if you spend it doing the right things. Team meetings will become productive and participative instead of dull or repetitive sessions where nothing of any importance takes place. Ideas will come from everywhere instead of only from you, and they will almost certainly be better ideas than you could have come up with on your own. So let's forget about putting some distance between ourselves and our teams and focus instead on getting the very best out of them by including them in as much strategic activity as we can.

This is not to suggest that we substitute decision-making with consultation as a matter of course, as that would be abdication of leadership and would be inconducive to respect and teamwork. Box 2 time may involve you explaining why you are making a particular decision and outlining the constraints you are working within so that everyone knows upfront what is and is not possible. You can then discuss the best way forward in the context of the parameters you have given them and save unnecessary confusion.

We cannot be good at everything, and may well have people in our team who are better at certain things than we are. Great – get them involved and make use of them! That's why I need people who are good with IT or administration, because I'm not. Find out what they are good at, find out what they enjoy, and involve them in that. If they are less confident about some things than others, that's fine because we all are: sometimes the answer will be to stop trying to do them; sometimes it will be to get as good at doing it as they can. Either way, knowing as much as possible about the team's priorities and challenges can only be good. Working with your team may not 'save' you any time, but it will make that time far more productive.

How do I delegate effectively?

When I was given my first director-level position, I was also given a PA. I thought that was pretty cool until one day she asked me if she could have a word. 'Yes, of course,' I said, 'what can I do for you?' I was taken aback when she said: 'You are making my job impossible!' She went on to explain that she was supposed to be organising me, but she couldn't do it properly because I kept my own diary, didn't keep her informed of my to-do list and kept doing things myself (such as booking train tickets, arranging conference tickets, typing up my own presentations). The result was a very demotivated personal assistant, who couldn't assist me and therefore had little job satisfaction. So I did what any sensible leader would do and asked her to tell me how I could put it right, and we arranged a weekly half-hour meeting that gave her all the information she needed to 'manage' me, saving me time and making me look better to the outside world. As a result I became more effective and she was happier and felt she was finally able to do her job. Sometimes we are our own worst enemy and have an impact on others that we are totally unaware of.

Delegation is the one behaviour that leaders and managers tell me they struggle with more than anything else. So what prevents us from letting go, even when we see the evidence all around us that we can't do everything on our own? There are some very real barriers to delegation, and we need to address these properly before we can list the benefits and force ourselves to do it.

Delegation is often misunderstood. It is not simply a matter of setting objectives and leaving someone else to do them. True delegation involves taking something that is normally in our own job role and handing it over to someone else to do instead. We are therefore giving that person something that we were previously responsible for. When we do that, are we delegating responsibility for that activity, or are we delegating the authority to do it?

Delegation is best understood as the process of handing over authority to someone else in a way that enables that person to make decisions usually made by the manager. However, you can delegate authority but you cannot delegate responsibility. In other words, you can delegate something in your job description and still retain the responsibility for it. If you hand over the responsibility, then there is a need to review it and include it in the other person's job description.

There are a number of 'symptoms' or warning signs that make it fairly clear that a manager needs to become an effective delegator. For example, you may need to delegate if you:

◆ Regularly work late or take work home

◆ Are unable to meet deadlines

◆ Avoid accepting help from others

◆ Devote time to operation and to detail (delivery), rather than to planning and controlling (strategy)

◆ Are experiencing reduced job satisfaction

◆ Have little or no confidence in the abilities of your colleagues.

If the team falls apart without you, with people unclear about what their responsibilities are, unaware of regular routines and deadlines or unsure how to perform key tasks, it's a fair bet that you are not an effective delegator. It is not a sign of effective management if the team cannot cope in your absence, or if you feel you have to do everything yourself in order to make sure it is done properly.

The following list shows the result of a syndicate exercise in a training course to identify the pros and cons of delegation as a management tool.

Why managers should delegate	*Why managers often avoid it*
Benefits of effective delegation	**Barriers to effective delegation**
Increases efficiency of the team	Uneasy about giving up 'power'
More time for 'thinking' and strategy	Being 'busy' is comfortable
Staff learning and development	Fear of no longer being the 'expert'
Staff motivation and achievement	Lack of trust in others' ability
Jobs you are delaying get done	They might show you up!
Increased team morale	They can do better without you
Reduced reliance on physical presence and input of manager	You are not as indispensable as you would like to be or to appear to be
Strengthens team capability	You might get the blame for someone else's poor performance
Increased staff autonomy	It takes too long to explain so you might as well do it yourself
Increased staff commitment	
Better value for money (cost of time)	You may give up something you enjoy
Establishes better relationships	You might not be able to give up something you hate!
Someone else may do it better	Staff might keep asking questions
Someone else may enjoy it more!	Staff might refuse to take on new tasks
Involves others = better ideas	

There are a number of good reasons for managers deciding not to delegate. These are not made up. However, they are all to a greater or lesser extent based on fear, and as we have seen a number of times during our journey, fear has no place in management. If we regard the barriers to delegating as based on a fear of what might happen if we let go, the answer is in how we see the process of delegation. If we are delegating authority, we retain the responsibility. This means that we are still in control: we decide to whom we delegate, what we delegate and how we delegate.

If we delegate in a Box 2 way (see page 89), we will delegate effectively, providing security for ourselves and the person we are delegating to. We can use delegation as a means of coaching and empowering people and see the time we put into the process as an investment in them and the performance of the whole team. The benefits listed in the positive column are worth having and produce real advantages for the team and the manager, so it is worth the initial discomfort of facing down the short-term and fear-based barriers that we may automatically erect. Follow these few suggestions for effective delegation and I can guarantee that your time and that of your team will be more effectively spent. Delegating well clearly qualifies as an investment in yourself and your team.

1. Be prepared to give up your favourites – don't simply give away jobs you hate!

2. Use delegation as a way of coaching and empowering people

3. Don't avoid delegating because it takes too long to teach people a new task – it will save you much more time in the end

4. Similarly, don't avoid delegating because you can do it better yourself *at the moment*

5. Make time for effective delegation – don't be a manager who leaves a scribbled list when they are about to go on leave for three weeks

6. Build in clear ground rules from the start: i.e. what level of authority are you delegating and what are the targets and timescales?

7. Also, build in arrangements for monitoring and review: this will give reassurance to you and your colleague, allowing you to keep control and giving your team member access to support and advice

8. Coach the team member by asking questions, seeking their solutions to problems and challenges and encouraging them to explain their reasons and assumptions

9. Acknowledge their ideas and recognise their performance – in other words, make sure that they are given credit for their achievements and support for their development.

The American author Michael E. Gerber, author of a series of books titled *E-Myth* (the 'E' stands for Entrepreneur), coined the now infamous phrase that too many people find themselves 'working in the business not on the business' to describe the tendency many of us have to get bogged down in the detail instead of looking at the bigger picture and thinking strategically. We must show some faith in our staff and allow them to work at a higher level than they currently are, to stretch them and equip them to take on more. This in turn frees us up to be more strategic and benefits everyone. Effective delegation, supporting personal growth for team members, is a great way to ensure that we give them the skills, knowledge and confidence to find things out for themselves and reduce the need for them to keep coming to us for solutions they could find for themselves.

Being indispensable is not important – indispensable managers stay where they are. Those who empower their teams, increase their commitment and develop their people are more likely to go on to be successful elsewhere.

How do I avoid taking work home with me (physically and/or mentally)?

If you habitually stay late every day or take work home every single night then it is fair to say you have a problem that needs addressing (unless you really enjoy it and actively choose to spend your time in this way). We all need to be flexible enough and committed enough to do those things when the situation demands but when it becomes a way of life then it is counterproductive. This behaviour is a sign that the job role is not properly resourced or clearly defined enough: either that or you are not doing it well enough in the time allowed, which this chapter should help you address.

Clear roles for you and your team members will go a long way towards addressing issues of resource and definition. Without these it is difficult for anyone to know how much is enough in terms of effort, time or results. Spend some time agreeing these aspects with everyone involved so you all know where you stand.

Clear targets and objectives that have been discussed, tested and agreed are also essential, otherwise you have no idea whether you are on the right track or not.

> *If you don't know where you're going, you'll end up*
> *somewhere else.*
>
> Yogi Berra

Regular monitoring and feedback are essential once you have a target in mind. Again, involve your team as fully as you can, and be prepared to receive feedback as well as give it. In fact, I suggest that actively seeking feedback (not in a needy, how-am-I-doing way) is a great way to validate others while learning and improving yourself.

Finally, my number one practical time management tip for you as a person is a very simple but highly effective one. As discussed, we can reduce the number of Box 3 interruptions (see page 89), principally by working with our team to use them as opportunities to engage with finding solutions and identifying improvements together. We cannot eliminate them altogether, however, and will only get frustrated if we think we can. I would like to close this chapter by asking you to try the following simple exercise.

At the end of your working day, before you leave your desk, have a look through your to-do list and identify the most important thing you want to achieve next. Then, write it on a Post-it note and place it where you will see it as soon as you sit down tomorrow. This becomes your focus for the day, then when the interruptions come and you answer your emails or take your phone calls, instead of sitting there shuffling paper and picking things up and putting them down as you flit between all the things that need doing, you simply return to your number one priority. Interruptions lose their power to completely derail you because they don't go on distracting you once you've dealt with them: you simply refocus and continue with what you were doing. You don't have to make a decision because it's already been made for you. All that remains is for you to complete the task.

Time Management for Managers: Takeaways from Chapter Six

♦ As a manager, your time management not only affects you, it directly impacts on how effective your team can be

♦ Seventy per cent of a manager's time is unplanned, dealing with issues and people that demand your attention now and get in the way of you achieving what you intended to do. This needs to be managed differently

♦ 'Box 2' time (see also page 89) is true management time: time for planning, monitoring and evaluation relationship building, organisation and research. We need to make time for this so we can be proactive and not simply react to whatever is thrown at us

♦ Interruptions and demands from others are annoying and disturb us, but we cannot ignore our colleagues – after all, we are paid to manage and work with them

◆ The best way to help everyone to be productive is not to separate yourself from your team in order to get your own work done, but to involve them in what you are thinking and doing. Bringing them into Box 2 with you (see also page 90) is the best way of doing this; it grows and empowers them, allowing you to delegate effectively and benefit from their ideas and knowledge

◆ Delegation is a vital behaviour for the effective manager but remember, you can delegate authority but you cannot give away your responsibility for the end result. Effective delegation helps everyone

◆ Planning and preparation are key to effective time management. If you don't know where you're going, you'll end up somewhere else!

7

Managing Change and Uncertainty

The need for change management

Change is constant. Every organisation and every team is in a state of flux, whether they realise it or not. Much of this is simply because we are in business and, in order to stay in business, we need to be able to respond to changes in the marketplace, in technology or even simply in fashion.

A successful team will be alert to these changes and ready to respond in an organised and constructive way. Better still, to be ahead of the game and anticipate change before our competitors so we give ourselves an advantage. The ultimate would be to identify the need for change before other people and to be proactive, leading positive or desirable change rather than simply reacting to it once the need has become so obvious that it cannot be ignored. One thing that is certain, however, is that no business or team is likely to prosper unless it continues to strive for improvement.

Innovation and change

There is more than one type of change, and there is a wealth of difference between change for its own sake and change for a reason. Some managers are tempted to make changes the moment they arrive in a new team or organisation, perhaps to get started immediately on what they have planned to do or possibly just to make their mark. Others may be tempted to leave well alone while they gather all the information they need, avoiding making hasty changes.

There is a balance to be struck between jumping straight in and holding back, and you will need to work out the best one for you and the situation. I would suggest that we avoid change for change's sake, and always have in mind the purpose of the change, so both you and your team have a clear understanding of what you are trying to achieve and why. Once you're clear and you have got your team behind you, then go for it!

Change is hard work but can also be tremendously rewarding. It's a great way to bring focus and energy to a team and an opportunity for you to both show leadership yourself and give others the chance to lead on their own areas of expertise or ability. Treat change initiatives as you would a project, giving them a beginning, middle and end. All projects are about change, whether that's improvement to an existing service or product, researching something or creating something new. Innovation is more powerful than change, and the best change always involves a bit of innovation. The most constructive way to manage a change process is therefore to inspire and motivate people by ensuring there is a shared goal that everyone understands and that, as far as possible, everyone is able to contribute to.

There are plenty of books on techniques for planning and implementing change, with details of tools and techniques including IT packages, Gantt charts and (my personal favourite) critical path analysis, but this is not the focus of this book. This chapter will help you to manage the most important and unpredictable part of any change process: people. For further reading, *The One Minute Manager* series by Kenneth Blanchard and Spencer Johnson is a good source of reference, as is Roger Plant's *Managing Change and Making It Stick* (see Bibliography, page 66).

The psychology of change

When told that they should expect some imminent change most people think first of all the negatives, but when asked what they want to happen in the future those same people will happily identify changes that they would like to see. If I put up the word 'change' in front of a group of delegates from any walk of life they will immediately focus on what they *don't* want to happen: words and phrases such as 'Why?' 'Oh no, not again!', or even 'What now?' are standard responses. Only after those thoughts and feelings are out of the way do they start to think that change could be a positive thing and begin to talk about 'challenge' or 'improvement' and consider that change could be 'interesting' or even 'exciting'.

> *We simultaneously seek change and avoid it. We want things to improve but hate to lose what we already have. Change brings with it risk and insecurity – two things we instinctively resist – so all too often when faced with change and uncertainty we withdraw to a safe place and protect ourselves by not engaging with the process of change.*

Change therefore produces an initial 'fear' response in people but it can also generate excitement and interest. We need to understand the nature of this knee-jerk fear response to change before we can successfully manage it. If we don't, we run the risk of this initial reaction preventing people from playing an active part as we try to make the change happen. We can't afford to allow this automatic instinct to 'keep things as they are' to turn into a longer-term fixed resistance to a change that we really need to happen.

Let's take a look at what causes this instinct in people to keep hold of what they have, even when logic would suggest that they could potentially have something very much better. We can then move on to consider how best to manage a change process to minimise resistance and promote enthusiasm.

The comfort zone and why change can be so uncomfortable

To a greater or lesser extent, we are all living in what could be described as our comfort zone. This is where we spend most of our time, doing all the things we usually do. The comfort zone is familiar and predictable: we know what to expect from our day and we know that we can cope with it. This is why people will put up with a job they don't enjoy, complain about it to their friends, criticise their bosses and operate at best on automatic. They know what they don't like; they may wish they had something better, but they won't do anything about it. They also know they can get up in the morning, feel unmotivated, and go home at the end of the day. It seems there is no real necessity to take any action.

It is possible to spend a very long time in this way, being unhappy with what you have but lacking the conviction to go anywhere else. In the workplace, this can breed low morale if the pervading mood is one of generalised, unspecific dissatisfaction. In most cases it is more likely that there is no real dissatisfaction at all, but there just isn't the energy or drive within the group to produce anything different or better. This is complacency. Everyone knows broadly what they are doing, and they do it, but there is little 'buzz' or creativity. In this environment, any ideas that do emerge are unlikely to get much of a hearing.

Change by its very nature threatens the status quo. Whether or not we like things as they are, we need a good reason to change them because by definition we know where we are, but we don't know where we're heading. The comfort zone is an important place for us, and people will often resist change simply because they feel safe where they are and to go anywhere else involves risk. As we have already seen, we avoid risk and seek security.

Anything that prevents us looking forwards will keep us looking back. So what are the perceived risks that can keep people where they are and prevent them from engaging with change? And what can we do to remove the fear element involved in taking those risks? Here are some of the most common fears of those facing change and uncertainty:

Fear of failure. We are conditioned to think that failing to achieve something means that we are a failure. Of course success is far preferable to failure, but it is unrealistic to think that we are going to succeed first time every time. Fear of failure is natural and human, but it is vital to overcome it as it has the potential to prevent us from trying in the first place.

In many situations if the prize is worth having then it is worth the risk of a few failures along the way. The American inventor and businessman Thomas Edison is the most widely quoted example of someone who built his success on failure – he claimed it took him 'literally thousands' of experiments with different materials before designing an effective filament for the first light bulb.

As individuals we need to be prepared to fail because failure is a necessary step on the road to success. As managers, we need to give our teams the confidence to occasionally fail without blaming themselves, blaming the management or blaming each other. In a process of change, failure is a risk we all take.

Fear of making a mistake. If you are asking your team to take on a new type of work, learn a new skill or change a familiar process then they are very likely to get it wrong the first time they try it. However, mistakes are not a problem as long as there are good support systems in place to deal with them. As we have learnt earlier, mistakes are part of the learning process and if we are too worried about getting the odd thing wrong then we will shy away from taking the calculated risks we need to take in order to make progress, learn a new skill or test alternatives.

> *'A man who never made a mistake never made anything.'*
>
> Henry Ford

Fear of losing status. We all value the skills and knowledge we have developed, and having 'expert' status within a team can be a source of real pride. If a change in priorities or the introduction of a new working practice means that the old way of doing things is no longer seen as valuable, it can be hard for the job holder to let go of their hard-earned status. Giving that person a role in introducing the new methods can be a great way of avoiding any feelings of irrelevance or loss, as can offering early training in the new skill set.

I remember one woman who was visibly upset because her desk had been moved from her favoured window seat to the far corner. She felt marginalised and could not accept that the move was not a personal insult to her. Her manager had not even thought about the impact on her, to the extent that he had even organised the move while she was on annual leave and so she returned to find that she had been 'exiled'.

Fear of the unknown. We need to feel secure at work in order to give our best, especially when decisions are being made that directly affect us. People like to be led; it helps them to feel safe. They also like to be involved, as it makes them feel wanted. As long as you have the authority to tell people what is going on, then you should tell them. Letting them know what is being proposed, why it is necessary and what the benefits will be are all effective ways of keeping people informed and involved. No one can be committed to something they don't understand.

These are all factors that may cause some to resist a change that you and/or your organisation regard as positive. However, perception is reality and if this is what people are feeling they will need the chance to share their concerns and resolve them.

The more someone feels pushed in one direction, the more likely they are to resist. This can take a number of forms. People can become obstructive and argumentative, but this kind of direct resistance is risky for a staff member as they may fear disciplinary action, so they are less likely to disobey instructions and more likely to simply refuse to cooperate in other ways. Once it becomes a 'battle', people are likely to suspect everything they are told, not come up with ideas and withdraw goodwill. This slows down progress and makes everything much more difficult.

While we as managers ultimately have the power to insist on a course of action, we are better advised to go to the 'resistors' and find out from them what the problems are. It may well be that we can provide reassurance or find a way to work things out together.

Making change happen – the Rubber Band Theory

We are more likely to work hard to make a change happen if we are motivated to achieve it. Typically, we are motivated either by resisting or achieving something. Whether the change happens successfully or not depends on whether we are committed to achieving it.

The theory works like this:

Whenever we are asked, forced into or wanting to consider a change, we are faced with tension between where we are now and where we want to be. The Rubber Band Theory pictures this tension as like a rubber band being stretched from two directions at once. In this case, it is being pulled in the direction of the new target at the same time as being stretched in the direction of the old way of doing things.

So what are the attractions or worries about each of these 'ends' of the rubber band?

Current state (Now)

1. What's good about it?

2. What's bad about it?

3. What will I gain by staying here?

4. What do I stand to lose if I leave it?

Future State (Goal)

1. What's good about it?

2. What's bad about it?

3. What will I gain by achieving it?

4. How much do I really want it?

Whether or not we achieve the change and get the results we are aiming for will depend entirely on whether we are committed to achieving it. The brain is uncomfortable with tension, so we want to resolve it as quickly as possible. If the pull of the current state is greater than that of the goal, we will be motivated to protect what we have and not to take any risks that might make things worse. On the other hand, if the pull of the goal is more powerful then we will be prepared to take the necessary risks to help us achieve it. The rubber band stretches as a result of the tension created by being pinned at two opposing points, eventually snapping at the weaker point and being propelled towards the strongest. The success of the change project therefore depends on which is the most attractive option to the team.

If we decide that it is easier or safer to stay where we are, we are likely to put limited effort into making the change and will tend to come up with all sorts of reasons to avoid it. Instead of working towards the goal, we will not be committed to it and will put all our efforts into staying where we are. In organisations this often translates into comments and attitudes such as: 'No one tells me anything', 'There's no point in doing it, they'll only change their minds again in a few weeks' or 'I think things should stay as they are; I bet they're only doing it so they can save money'.

If the goal we are aiming for is positive enough to make us want to achieve it then we will work towards it with focus and anticipation. So, all you have to do is to make sure that there is a good enough reason for your team to go for it. The chances of success for any change project are greatly improved if there is genuine enthusiasm for the end result. Therefore, the pull of the 'desired future state' needs to be greater than the pull of staying where you are. No matter how committed people are to the organisation or team, they are usually most concerned with their own interests. Hopefully, you will be able to demonstrate to them that the interests of the company and the individual are one and the same, but the overriding interest for everyone and the question that needs to be answered clearly and powerfully is this one: *'What's in it for me?'*

In the example of my team in Chapter Five (see also page 63), it was a joint decision to be the best in the country, with the prize being the satisfaction of a measurable achievement. We responded to the challenge of achieving a really stretching target and creating a buzz around doing something well outside our normal routine. In the case of the charity described in Chapter Two (see also page 48), the current state was deeply unattractive and the desired future state would have seemed like a dream when they first discussed their options. Common to both of these case studies was the rejection of the current state (complacency in our case and disaster in theirs) combined with the attraction of a clearly defined goal.

Managing change

The most important factor in determining our attitude towards change is whether we think that the change is within or outside our control. The more we understand about the change process, the less scary we perceive it to be. If we think that the change is being done to us, we will want to resist it. This can take a number of forms, such as denying that the change is happening, refusing to get involved, getting angry about it or (and this is possibly the hardest reaction for a manager to deal with) pretending to accept it by going through the motions.

If we think that we can influence the change process we have a reason to get involved in it. Involving someone means that they have a role to play and can make a difference to the outcome.

Successful change depends on managing the process aspects of the change project, including proper planning, clear objectives and adequate resources. However, in order for organisational change to deliver the results we want, it is vital that we handle the people side of the equation well enough to get them fully on board.

Managing change in an organisation involves working with the people who are (a) affected by the change in some way and (b) whom we are relying on to make the change happen. This does not mean that we are delegating our decision-making to them or that everyone has to agree with what is being proposed. It is always going to be the job of the senior management of an organisation or the leader of a team to make the ultimate decisions. What it does mean is that the people who are going to actually implement the change need to be given the opportunity to understand what is going on and feel involved.

In the 1940s the German-American psychologist Kurt Lewin identified three key stages of successful change management in groups and his theory is probably the simplest and neatest of all change theories, consisting of three words:

UNFREEZE

↓

CHANGE

↓

REFREEZE

This theory suggests that if you impose a change too quickly, missing out on the consultation and investigation phase, people will feel they have been kept in the dark. They will naturally be suspicious for all the reasons we have already highlighted and, as a result, this will only reinforce their need to defend themselves by retreating into their comfort zone.

If those affected can't ask questions and don't understand the rationale for the change being imposed on them, they will resist it. This makes it much more likely that those introducing the change will resort to top-down approaches in order to enforce the change on a now reluctant and resentful team. This is a failure of management.

In order to effectively engage with a change process people need to know:

1. Why the change is necessary (what's the point?)

2. How it will affect them

3. How it might benefit them or the organisation

4. What they will need to do.

People need information. If they are kept in the dark about something, they will not feel part of it. If people (management, in this case) don't tell them what is going on, they are likely to make it up – this is how rumours start, and rumours lead to conspiracy theories and people getting upset about things that may not even be happening. As a manager or leader, we can avoid a lot of this by being clear with people about the four questions we have just listed.

Unfreeze. As we begin the change process we need to recognise that there is an existing structure still in place. People are used to working in the way they are, and they are used to the set of priorities they are currently working towards. There are vested interests, there is inertia and there is, of course, the comfort zone, all of which will cause people to question the need for change.

Unfreezing is the essential process of discussion and debate. We need to give people information, invite questions and create a picture of the benefits of the change we are proposing. They must be given some time to weigh up the pros and cons of the suggested change and decide that change is in fact both necessary and desirable, or, at the very least, inevitable. Crucially, they understand why it is happening. Only once they have reached this level of understanding can they consider how to get involved in the change process itself.

Change or Transition. This is where the change begins to happen. Your role as manager is to keep feeding people with information, keep answering their questions and keep discussing progress. You can involve the team in planning and you should be providing them with any necessary training, coaching and support.

Remember that while you may know the answers to their questions yourself, no one else will know until somebody takes the time to tell them. Each individual needs to know the answer to that most basic of questions: 'What's in it for me?' Once they know, they will be more interested in getting involved. By the way, even if they don't like the change, they will understand it and know what to expect, and that will remove the confusion that can so easily undermine even the most positive or necessary change.

Keep reinforcing the big picture – in other words, what is the reason for the change, what are the benefits for everyone, and what will the future look like? Answering these questions is the only way to melt the ice rather than break it. Once we have melted it, we can then work together to create the new shape and freeze that into place.

Refreeze. If the previous two stages have been managed well then the end result should be that we have successfully introduced the new 'shape' whether that is a new product, an improved process or a commitment to a new target.

We began this chapter by saying that change is constant so we need to be careful about claiming anything is frozen in a permanent new way of doing things. Once the change has been implemented, it needs to be continually reinforced in order to maintain the new focus we have decided on. This means demonstrating that we are achieving the objectives we agreed and delivering the agreed benefits, so it is important here that the end result contains monitoring and measurement to check that we are on track and make any further necessary changes.

In summary, take people with you; give them time to ask questions and to come to terms with the new situation. Be as open as you can with information on the reason for the change and the likely impact on them. If you don't have all the answers, then say so with a promise that you will keep them informed and don't pretend everything is all right unless you know it is. It is essential throughout any period of change that the team is able to trust its leader, even if you can't always provide the reassurance they need.

Managing negative change

Not all change is positive, and some change is very difficult to argue in favour of. You may well be asked to be the face of a change that you either actively oppose or at least regret the necessity for. While the behaviours for managing this type of change are very similar to those outlined in this chapter, there are additional issues to deal with.

Firstly, you may need to manage your own response. Assuming you are not so opposed to the change that you feel compromised enough to resign over it, you need to be able to separate your personal feelings from your professional responsibility. Have your debate within the management team, then leave your misgivings behind you. You will serve your team best if you manage the process well, rather than winding people up further by criticising the organisation and adding to any feelings of anger or injustice.

Stay calm and rational. Your job is to help your team come to terms with the change in their own way, so you need to be clear and honest about what you know and give them the time to process the new situation.

Offer support. Be there for them, in whatever way they need. This may involve listening even when there is nothing practical you can do. Also, offer practical support if asked for it.

Answer their questions. People need information, so answer any questions they have. If you don't know the answer, tell them so and take their questions to the decision-makers.

Create trust. If you say you will do something, do it. If you can't do it, tell them honestly. Follow-up is crucial.

Be approachable. Remember, you are the conduit between the change instigators and those affected. You may be the only person they can directly speak to throughout the process.

Problem or opportunity? You decide!

At times we all wish for a life without problems, but if we wish for that then we wish for a life of boredom and frustration. We need problems to provide the impetus for change and growth by giving us an imperative to do something different. My favourite definition of a problem is that *a problem is a situation requiring action* – we need to do something about it. 'Doing something' requires most of the activities that make for effective management such as research, analysis, monitoring, evaluation, decision-making, consultation, creativity, focus, goal setting, action and identifying and implementing change. All the things that make this job worthwhile!

Nothing was ever improved without someone imagining a better outcome, planning to do it and getting it done. If you have taken the trouble to create a proper team, given them a focus and built up their confidence, then problems become opportunities to change things, to stretch themselves, to be creative and to make improvements. Nothing grows unless it has to overcome difficulties and adapt. This is why the Chinese use the same character to describe the concepts of both problem and opportunity. As another proverb says, the problem contains the seeds of its own solution.

Change is a fundamental part of management: we are an agent of change. We monitor, evaluate, consult, make decisions and motivate people to achieve and improve. We are not paid to sit and watch the wheels turn, we are paid to make them go faster, or run more efficiently, or to steer them so they take our team and our organisation to the right destination.

Managing Change and Uncertainty: Takeaways from Chapter Seven

♦ Whether we like it or not, change is constant

♦ Change is a process and like any other process, it needs to be managed

♦ Most people instinctively resist change, even when they want a better life

♦ If people feel that change is out of their control, or being done to them rather than with their involvement, then they tend to avoid it. When they are involved in the process, understand and can influence it, they are more likely to engage with it.

♦ Not all change is positive for people, or they may have very good reasons for resisting it. We need to give them time to come to terms with unwelcome change, time to ask questions and time to adjust.

8

Managing Difficult People and Situations

What do we mean by a difficult person?

One of the most challenging parts of leadership is dealing with 'difficult' people. I have lost count of the number of managers who have lamented the existence of one or more difficult persons and expressed the wish that they could somehow be surgically removed from their team and workplace. One person can effectively destroy a whole team or even a small organisation. They can ruin your day, your week or even your entire job. If you are aiming to enjoy your job, and if you want your team to enjoy theirs, you simply cannot allow this to happen.

People try to exert power or control over their environment for any number of reasons. If they can't do it positively, they may well try to do it negatively and, with practice, they can become very good at doing it. Your job is to recognise the signs, understand the reasons and take the necessary action to either turn the difficult person around, or firmly and decisively show them the door. Failure to do so will impact on you and the rest of your organisation.

We all have someone who springs to mind when we think of difficult people, but what do we mean by a difficult person?

Someone who disagrees with us or doesn't cooperate? Who sabotages, or who we can't handle? Is it a result of their personality or their situation? Or is it just that they fail to do what we want them to do and therefore we experience them as obstructive or antagonistic?

For a manager, it is someone who is not responding to what we are trying to do to help them, challenge them and get them contributing. Our job is to find out why, if we can, and work out how to get the best out of them. If we can't turn them around – and we can't be successful every time – then for our own peace of mind and our own protection, we need to know that we have done everything we can for them, the team, the organisation, the customer and any other stakeholders.

How not to be a difficult person yourself

The first rule of handling difficult people is to understand that we cannot control the actions of other people; all we can do is control ourselves. Fortunately, that is also the most powerful thing we can do. By changing our own behaviour we give the other person something different to contend with, so they have to react to what we do and don't have the field entirely to themselves. As we'll see in the sections below on 'game playing' and assertiveness, we need to remain in control of ourselves if we are to stand any chance of staying in control of any given situation.

As a manager you are responsible for what happens in your team and for getting the results for which you and your team are employed, so it is necessary for you to retain control. Use the word 'responsibility' if you prefer: you are the responsible person so you need to take responsibility for the outcome. However, this is easier said than done when you are in conflict with another person and there are difficult issues to be resolved and harsh things being said or felt.

If we strive to be emotionally intelligent and to listen to others before leaping in with our own opinions then, most of the time, we will do better than if we allow our feelings to get the better of us and become too personally involved. It's difficult to do, but the best results for us in terms of both our performance and our well-being will be gained by being professional and remembering that this is a work environment and we are paid to do our job and get things done. That said, we can still do more to ensure that we are, in the time-honoured phrase, 'part of the solution and not part of the problem'.

Be clear. It's no use complaining that we've told someone the same thing over and over again but they still don't 'get it'. If they haven't understood you then they won't have got it and they won't be able to do it. Instead of assuming you have made yourself clear, take a few moments to check that what you've said has been properly understood. People perceive and understand things in different ways, so you may need to vary your delivery, or you may need to change the medium.

Some easy ways to check understanding include the following:

◈ Ask someone to say in their own words what they understood from you

◈ Invite them to show you their first attempt at doing what you've asked

◈ Reinforce your message through coaching and feedback.

Be consistent. Avoid giving mixed messages. If you want someone to believe that something is important, behave as if it *is* important. Don't announce something once and then forget about it until you spot a problem. Remember the old adage that what gets measured gets delivered, so if you want your team to think of something as a priority then treat it as such by asking about it, inviting ideas and information and providing updates.

People like predictability in their bosses, so make sure that you are always the same in your dealings with them. This doesn't mean being boring and never surprising them; you don't want them to become complacent about your leadership but you do want them to feel safe. You need to give consistent messages on priorities, standards and behaviour. Also, you need to manage your mood so that your team don't have to get used to dealing with you in unpredictable moods: if something is right or wrong one day, it should be the next. You are human, but you are also professional.

Professional behaviour, particularly for leaders, is a performance. It is not an actor's performance, but more like that of a musician. Whatever pressures you might be under, play the right notes; your colleagues need the best version of you.

Be calm. If you lose your cool, you've lost your argument and, with it, the moral high ground. Certain people will always aim to get under your skin, so don't reward them: if you stay calm, you can think, which is priceless.

Be fair. Respect is more important than popularity and fairness more powerful than revenge. Decide what the right thing is and do it. Don't be deflected by the understandable urge to punish those who anger you, to ask only those you know will say yes or to avoid those who will say no. You have a right to expect everyone to perform to agreed standards and to pull their weight on behalf of the rest of the team.

Sell benefits, not features. If you are seeking to influence someone, remember to get to know them and their needs first. They will buy what is of value to them more readily than what is of value to you or anyone else. Once you have taken the time to get to know your team member you will have a better idea about what means something to them and you can tap into it. This may be status, learning, progression or the easy life, but at least if you know what it is then you will be able to speak their language.

Reward the right behaviour. Managing people can be a complex task, but there's no benefit in making it more difficult than it needs to be. People need and want attention. Some seek it legitimately but others seek it for the wrong reasons. I have seen many a manager fall into the trap of giving all their time and attention to the difficult person while largely ignoring those who are working hard and contributing well. This reinforces the wrong behaviour. If you were training a dog and asked it to sit and it ran around barking, would you chase after it with a treat? No, you wouldn't. Reinforce good behaviour so attention is earned through performance. Not politically correct maybe, but still worth remembering.

Never try to appease. Appeasement gets you nowhere. If you give concessions to people who have done nothing to deserve them then they will take those concessions and demand more: when given away cheaply, concessions are not valued by those who receive them. Instant gratification is short-lived, while deferred gratification is valued because it was earned. This is why I prefer to link any team activity such as a team meal, cake or away-day planning event (my teams know how to live!) to an achievement or recognition of effort.

How do I manage or avoid conflict?

Conflict is not necessarily a bad thing. In fact, in many ways it's an essential part of the mix in an effective and productive team. Without some degree of conflict there is no opportunity for people to ask the hard questions that need to be asked as a team works towards its goal; no chance to challenge orthodoxies or habits that are getting in the way of innovation; no way to debate alternative methods of getting things done.

The question is not whether we should allow conflict in our team, because we should: the important thing is the nature of the conflict. Conflict based on ego and self-interest is not constructive because it is not aiming to reach a solution that benefits the team, the organisation or the customer. However, conflict based on finding a better way to do things, disagreement about method, values or objectives is often necessary and produces real benefit in the form of renewed commitment, increased understanding and greater clarity.

In his excellent book, *Good To Great*, Jim Collins found that honest and often uncomfortable disagreements were a regular and essential feature of the most successful organisations. His research team concluded that the right people, with the right motives and the right level of commitment, would often find themselves in conflict precisely because they cared about their work. These conflicts could be loud and long, but they were never personal.

They would only end with agreement on the right way forward, and that agreement would only be reached once the challenges had been faced with honesty and courage and the best solution found. In these organisations, conflict led to greater focus and increased commitment, so conflict in itself is not a problem; it only becomes a problem if the motive for that conflict is wrong or if it is avoided because we find it difficult to manage.

This makes our job easier. If the conflict we are experiencing is a result of people in our team attempting to get better results for the organisation by challenging ineffective methods and asking difficult questions, then we can encourage and facilitate that conflict. Such conflict is great: it is professional and necessary. If, on the other hand, the conflict is the result of individuals seeking to gain an advantage over others, following their own personal agenda at the expense of the team or in any way undermining the team's ability to achieve its objectives, then the conflict this behaviour causes is negative and needs to be challenged and stopped in its tracks.

The Thomas-Kilmann Conflict Mode Instrument (great name!) is a questionnaire developed by two leading thinkers on conflict and working relationships. First published in 1974, its developers were Ralph H. Kilmann and Kenneth W. Thomas, who developed the instrument at UCLA. In it, they identify five ways in which people typically respond to conflict. It's worth going through these to flag up the strengths and weaknesses of these approaches, and when they may or may not be appropriate. The following are my own thoughts on these behaviours and should not be seen as representative of the findings of the authors of the Instrument.

Avoidance. Avoiding is generally seen as a negative behaviour, particularly in relation to handling difficult people or situations, but it very much depends on the context. It can perhaps best be summed up by the phrase 'pick your battles'. If you avoid a necessary conflict in which there is a lot to lose then clearly avoiding it is not an option, but if the conflict is of little importance then why waste precious time or resources fighting it? Also, prevention is better than cure, so if the relationship is more important than the specific issue at stake then it may be right to take a step back. Use this approach when there is nothing to be gained from the fight.

Accommodating. This is an approach that places low emphasis on your own needs and high emphasis on the needs of the other person. At best accommodating shows low ego and can help build trust in a relationship, but at its worst it could show low self-worth and make you appear to be an easy 'opponent' if your colleague sees the relationship as a competitive one. This can be useful in negotiation as part of a package of agreements but you need to be sure that you are giving away something of little value to yourself and of high value to them.

Competing. In the transactional analysis model this is a clear 'Win:Lose' approach. A person using the competing style in conflict situations is someone who wants to win. It is a high-ego, low-cooperation behaviour where only one outcome is sought. If winning is important, then a determined competitor may well put themselves in a good position to win and to build a reputation for being a tough opponent, but there is a cost. If you win using this style then your adversarial approach is unlikely to make you first choice for anyone wishing to share information, feelings or to work together. By making the issue a straight fight and putting your success at front and centre, if you lose then you tend to lose big.

Compromising. In a negotiation the formula 'If you ... then I' is an effective one. At its most useful, compromise means that with a bit of movement on each side you achieve an acceptable result for both. However, you are unlikely to make a significant creative breakthrough using this approach as it depends on a bit of trimming here and there in order to reach a compromise solution. By its very nature, a compromise solution will not allow you everything you want but it does enable you to move forward, having found a way around a difficult issue.

Collaborating. Often considered to be the best outcome of all, collaboration can mean that by working together two parties can come up with a better solution than either would have been able to reach on their own. The ideal scenario is that there is a coming together that makes use of the different perspectives, abilities and knowledge of both to develop a new approach. At best, this is what true collaboration achieves. However, there are drawbacks to collaboration as it can be time consuming and resource intensive, making it an expensive process: if we habitually seek collaboration in any conflict situation then we may waste time and effort over something that could have been dealt with more efficiently by, say, compromise or avoiding the debate in the first place.

For me the main value of the Thomas-Kilmann model is to increase awareness of the available approaches, recognise our own preferences and choose when and where each style would be most appropriate instead of simply behaving as we always do. The strengths of each approach become apparent when it is used in the right situation, while the drawbacks are found when we apply it automatically without regard to the end result we are looking for.

The assertive manager (theory)

Assertiveness is best understood in the context of stress, conflict and working with difficult people and situations. We can all manage when things are going well, we can all behave assertively when there is nothing much to be assertive about, and we can all take decisions when there is little riding on the outcome. It is when there are problems that we earn our money.

Most people are aware of the three behaviours described in assertiveness theory: aggressive, assertive and passive. Assertiveness has its roots in transactional analysis (TA), as both are based on the importance of the state of mind with which we approach relationships with others.

An aggressive person and a passive person appear at first sight to be very different characters. We associate different behaviours with each state – for example, we would expect an aggressive person to be loud, opinionated, perhaps bullying, threatening or offensive. By contrast we would expect a passive person to be quiet, submissive and to back off in the face of contradiction or criticism. Very different behaviours, but both spring from the same instincts and are an attempt to shield the individual from the same worries and concerns. The root of these very different behaviours is often some form of self-doubt, with accompanying low self-esteem and, therefore, confidence. All the individuals are doing is protecting themselves in their very different ways.

In TA terminology the aggressive personality is going for a 'Win:Lose' response to a stressful situation and the more stressed and fearful they become, the more aggressively they are likely to behave. The passive person is protecting themselves in the opposite way: going for a 'Lose:Win' outcome and in effect saying to their perceived challenger, 'You win, now go away'. Both of these are emotional reactions to what they see as a threat from outside and both fear exposure for what they see as their weaknesses. Therefore both put up their defences to make sure they are not breached and are not forced to deal with the root cause of their low self-esteem.

The assertive person is different from the other two personas in several important ways.

Assertiveness is logical, not emotional. An assertive response to a difficult situation is not an emotional one. There is no need for emotion because the ego is not involved. If, for example, someone disagrees with an aggressive person then they will see it as an insult and will become aggressive as a way of defeating their challenger. This is because a challenge from someone else must be beaten to avoid being exposed as weak or vulnerable. An aggressive person cannot afford to be wrong. If someone disagrees with a passive person then they will probably back down and cease to argue their case.

Assertiveness is learnt, not instinctive. The instinctive response to a threat is to defend yourself but an assertive person does not see the need to do so as they do not see disagreement as a threat. They have learnt that there is a more effective way to handle the situation and that is on its merits. Very few of us are naturally assertive but we can learn and become more skilled in assertive attitudes and behaviour.

Assertiveness focuses on the solution, not the problem. The drive for the other two behaviours is self-protection: they are inward-looking. Assertiveness is outward-facing and solution-focused. What matters to an assertive person is that all involved work together to achieve the best possible result in any given situation.

Assertiveness is stable, not fragile. Because the other two states are emotional, defensive and instinctive, they are inherently unstable. This can lead to the phenomenon of the passive-aggressive swing, in which people go in an instant from apparent confidence to a complete mess, or from submissiveness to verbal or physical violence. This is why assertive behaviour, such as the 'adult' behaviour described in Chapter Two (see also page 24), is stronger than the alternatives.

The assertive manager (practice)

So what does all the above mean when it comes to handling difficult people and situations? Firstly, look into assertiveness in a serious way if you haven't already done so and work on your ability to deal with both the aggressive and passive personality types. Secondly, although I have provided a simplified version of the theory here, remember these are signposts and can only be (useful, I hope!) caricatures of the complex people you work with.

Avoid triggering their defence mechanism unnecessarily. Make use instead of the advantages of being an assertive communicator by asking good questions, listening with interest and helping them to consider the impact of their behaviour on their own goals. If a person is given the opportunity and space to come up with their own solutions without feeling the need to defend themselves (either through attack or submission) then they are more likely to reach a logical conclusion than an emotional one.

Avoid the temptation to step in early and present a solution if they are not ready for it. There are a number of benefits to avoiding being the 'rescuer'. The rescuer can quickly become the persecutor in the mind of your 'victim'. As soon as your solution looks like failing, you are there as a convenient target for their blame and responsibility.

Your responsibility is to the performance of the team and to manage individuals effectively. Their responsibility is to work with you to help you achieve that. Don't make yourself responsible for them outside of their work performance.

Confront problems early on. The worst kind of conflict is the type that rumbles on without resolution. If you notice something, act on it. This may mean having difficult conversations at times and making difficult decisions. Saying 'no' is never comfortable but sometimes necessary. There is always a short and long-term implication of any decision you make. When denying someone or reinforcing an unpopular decision there is a golden rule in operation: if you take the easy way out, it will be more pleasant in the short term but will come back and bite you in the long term. It is better to brave some immediate negative consequences for doing the right thing than to court temporary relief by putting it off – short-term pain really is worth it for long-term gain.

Responsibility without power: don't take it. If we shirk our responsibilities in the hope of an easier life, we still don't escape those responsibilities. Instead we are left with the trappings of power but none of the benefits. The trappings include the right to be blamed for whatever is done in our name.

Power without responsibility: don't allow it. This is the flip side of the previous point, in which the manager's abdication places power in the wrong hands. That's not to say that placing power in the team's hands is a bad thing in itself – in fact, it's a great thing so long as it's deliberate on our part, it's the right team members with the right motivation and we have equipped them to do it. The risk is that weak or absent leadership allows people to take the lead but not the responsibility that should go with it.

The games people play

Here, I would like to say a few words about the professional game-players who seem to crop up in many workplaces (and elsewhere). In his perceptive book, *Games People Play: The Psychology of Human Relationships*, Dr Eric Berne identifies a number of 'games' that are often played at the expense of unwitting colleagues. They have intriguing titles such as 'If only, then I' and 'Why don't you? ...Yes, but'.

'If only I didn't have this wooden leg, I would have been a dancer'. 'If only they recognised my talent here, I would get promotion'. Statements such as these are intended to provoke sympathy and pave the way for the next game, 'Why don't you? ... Yes, but'. In this game you offer them a series of suggestions to help them overcome their lack of opportunity. Each suggestion is then dismissed as impossible, irrelevant or inappropriate. The game dictates that any suggestion you make is met by an example of why it will not work. As the unwitting 'rescuer' you are then led into making further suggestions, which will also be rejected. The pay-off for the game-player is therefore more attention, more sympathy and less responsibility. S/he can continue to be a victim of society, the world, fate, their colleagues and, of course, you.

Why play these games? Berne's answer is that there is always a pay-off for a serial game-player. In the case of the above examples, the players get sympathy and attention, which are quite nice things to have. They also take away any need for responsibility or action on their part, as all the suggestions come from other people and they can happily reject them all as unobtainable. If you keep hearing 'yes, but' every time you suggest something to help someone then you are in the hands of a game-player.

The final game, titled 'Ain't it awful?', is the good old moaning club. Whatever happens is criticised and evidence found to prove that the company, the manager or the customer cannot be trusted or simply doesn't know what they are doing. The pay-off here is an excellent one: the other members of the club agree with you on every point, so you get validation for your insight without having to lift a finger. This is real power without responsibility.

These games are impossible to win. The players are experts in their field and their logic is circular. They definitely count as difficult people. Help!

There's only one way to combat these games: don't play them! Games need more than one player and that player is supposed to follow the rules. So don't join in. Once you've recognised that you're being played, or that colleagues are being sucked in, stop playing.

If you continue to play, you are only rewarding them for the wrong behaviour. Whatever you try to do will be incorporated into the game. Lose your temper? They're a victim. Offer suggestions? You're putting pressure on them. Offer sympathy? You're giving them attention. But if you stop doing those things, they will need to change tack in order to get the same pay-offs. They will have to stop playing too. Now, you can talk.

Managing Difficult People and Situations: Takeaways from Chapter Eight

♦ Don't be a 'difficult' person yourself! Remember, your behaviour leads directly to their behaviour

♦ Reward the right behaviour. Give your time, attention and credit for doing the right things, not the wrong ones

♦ Not all conflict is bad. Conflict based on ego and self-interest is unhealthy conflict in a team, but conflict based on finding a better way to achieve things, disagreement about method, values or objectives is often necessary and produces a better result than not facing up to these things

♦ Appeasement gets you nowhere. If you give concessions to people who have done nothing to deserve them, they will take those concessions and then demand more. Concessions given away cheaply are not valued by those who receive them

♦ There's a range of approaches to handling conflict – we need to be skilled in all of them and able to select the right method for the right situation

♦ Don't allow yourself to be manoeuvred into having responsibility without power

♦ Similarly, don't allow others to have power without responsibility.

9

Managing Your Manager

Why do I need to manage my manager?

If you are trying to manage your manager, and it is an essential skill if you really want to get anything done, then you need to brush up on some specific influencing skills. This chapter takes you through the benefits of managing your manager and gives you some ideas for getting the best out of him or her. Some important elements we will explore include putting yourself in their shoes, talking their language, pain and pleasure revisited, and coming to them with solutions, not problems.

A common complaint from middle managers is that although they know what they want to do, they know they could do it and their team is in full support of their ideas, they can't get past their line manager. This can be frustrating for individual managers and for their teams and, if a pattern is established where apparently valid arguments are consistently ignored, then it can ultimately put people off coming up with ideas in the first place. No fresh ideas means no development, and no development means no improvement: if you are a senior manager, this could be about you!

Lack of support from higher management can also undermine your attempts to deal with a problem decisively. For example, if you have exhausted all other options with a difficult member of staff and have taken a decision to refuse a request or insist on certain standards then you may well need the support of your line manager. Just like children, people seeking to push boundaries can spot divisions between the parent figures and turn them into opportunities to spread confusion or indecision.

Walk a mile in my shoes

We need to be careful before making assumptions about the behaviour of senior leaders and, as with any temptation to leap to judgement, it's a good idea to check that we understand where the other person is coming from. If it's important to get to know and understand your team before attempting to influence them, it's no different when it comes to influencing your own manager. In order to work effectively with our line managers, and to build a good working relationship with them, we need to understand their motivations, their concerns and their priorities.

As a senior manager who has held director-level positions in the public, private and community sectors I have a lot of respect for the pressures and responsibilities of high-level leadership. The higher up the chain we go, the more visible we are and the fewer hiding places we have – it goes with the territory.

Senior leaders are often time-starved and overloaded with complex and conflicting demands. Just like you, they are pressured from above and below, with the added element of increased accountability for their departments or organisations. They need to be excellent time managers. They also need to be well supported by effective systems and processes within the organisation. Sometimes the demands of the job make it hard to focus on any one thing for long enough to deal with it properly; sometimes they are simply not very good at managing their time.

In other words, they have all of the same issues as you do, and would relate to everything we've discussed throughout this book. In such a role, it is inevitable that some things are going to drop off their radar from time to time and one such thing is frequently their continuing role as a people manager. That means managing and supporting you can sometimes slip down their list. This is not personal and can be seen as a backhanded compliment, as they don't need to worry about you and your team.

When someone is that busy, and is looking in so many different directions, it's easy for them to miss what is going on under their noses. Many leaders in this position revert to managing by exception, so if they don't hear from you then they assume there is no problem. On one level it makes perfect sense, as they have to spread their resources (time, energy, focus) thinly. But on another level, this can lead to a number of problems for them and those who work for them, as follows.

Isolation. Although it could be less efficient in terms of getting things done myself, I always preferred to have my desk in the main office rather than in an office of my own. The benefits far outweighed the drawbacks, I found, as I could be involved in what was going on, I was available to my colleagues and there was more of a sense of working together. I could be more responsive to developments and it enabled my teams to be more proactive.

This isn't always possible, particularly when there are split sites or field workers, in which case it becomes essential to have regular contact such as phone calls and diarised face-to-face meetings whenever practical. As a middle manager it is important for you to do your bit to keep this level of contact up. A regular feed of information to your line manager, such as results, completed actions and highlighted issues and opportunities, reassures them that you are delivering and helps build trust – even if they don't read most of it!

An apparent lack of interest. If your line manager seems to pay attention only when there is a problem, then it can lead you to think that he or she is not really interested, but this is very unlikely to be the case. We all need recognition for the contribution we make and managing by exception denies us this feedback.

Again, providing your manager with good news can be a useful exercise, even if it is just copying them in on email updates you send out to your team. When you come to make a recommendation or present a business case then you have something to refer to and some credibility behind you already.

Problems create opportunity. If your line manager is distant and discourages openness and engagement, then he or she is missing out on potentially invaluable learning for everyone as solving problems is a great way to grow and learn. Preventing problems through analysing results and the reasons behind them, good or bad, is even better. As we investigate and understand performance, we identify opportunities for further development and improvement.

If your line manager is not doing this with you, you need to do it with your own team and communicate any findings upwards. This is the raw material for your business case that you will need to make when introducing a new idea.

Influencing your manager

You need to spend time getting to know your line manager as a person, assuming they will allow you to do so, but what follows is some advice on approaching your manager on important issues, which is broadly applicable.

Bring them solutions, not problems. A bit of a cliché but still one of the best pieces of advice I can give you: managers don't like whingers, so try to avoid going to them with anything that sounds like a complaint or an admission of weakness. (If you have a great relationship with your line manager based on honesty and they actively coach and develop you, then you have an excellent manager and don't need this section.)

Given the environment in which senior leaders work with boards, accountants and senior management meetings to answer to, it can come as little surprise if some learn to become risk averse, ending up suggesting reviews or asking for more detailed proposals instead of joining in with your enthusiasm. They are worried about taking the blame when it goes wrong – better to do nothing and let braver souls take the risks.

If you need their agreement or support for something you want to do then take the time to prepare a good business case. For the reasons outlined above, managers are conditioned to look for the flaws in any proposal that may expose them to problems in the future. Leaders hate to be associated with failure and have an eagle eye for risk. A well-researched business case with projections based on evidence will go a long way towards giving them the reassurance they need.

Clarify boundaries and expectations. An absent or distant manager can be a good thing as long as you have gained their trust. The difficulty comes when you are denied support but also denied the freedom to make decisions and sort things out for yourself. This is a case where you need to establish some clear boundaries. Job descriptions should be the place to do this, reinforced by effective supervision meetings or other regular reviews.

If your job description is out of date or clearly inadequate for your role then this is an opportunity to make a helpful change. A good job description should contain not only a clear outline of what you are required to do, but also what you are *not* required to do. Establish some ground rules with your line manager that make clear to both of you when you are able to act on your own and when you need to refer upwards.

Build in monitoring and review responsibilities and also what information needs to be collected, who needs to see it and how it will be used in decision-making. The more clearly these elements are set out in advance, the less opportunity for confusion and delay later as you know where you stand, you have it in writing, and you can refer to it for guidance instead of waiting to get permission from your manager.

It's no good for either of you if you have to go to your manager all the time for the authority to act. After all, you are both doing what you think best for the organisation, so if you are agreed on the goal then you should feel free to take action within your level of responsibility. When it comes to doing what you believe is right, so long as it is within the agreed boundaries, my approach is always to ask forgiveness rather than permission.

Talk their language. Once you've found out what makes them tick and know what is important to them, talk their language. They will not be influenced by what you want or by what your team may be asking for, but by what will give them the outcomes they need. This doesn't mean that you need to give up on your initiative; just be aware of who is listening to your business case. You might be convinced and your team may be right behind you, but you are no longer the people who need convincing.

If your manager is interested in saving money they won't be keen to hear you suggest making an expensive purchase. You may be proposing a very sensible investment that will save money in the medium term, so focus instead on the potential savings rather than the expense. Your manager is interested in making savings, not committing further expenditure.

If they are being judged on sales then they may not be interested in a 2 per cent improvement in quality. Instead of focusing on the quality issue you will need to show the impact that an improvement in quality will make in terms of sales and productivity.

Build trust. Nothing convinces a senior manager to listen to you more than a proven track record of being right a few times before. That's why it is important for you to make them aware of success stories and the benefits you are producing for the organisation and, by extension, for your manager.

This behaviour doesn't come naturally to most of us; we see any form of self-publicity or self-satisfaction as a bit unsavoury and embarrassing, just as we brush off compliments as not being deserved. It's a very British thing. Interestingly, in Jim Collins' book, *Good To Great*, the research team found that the most successful business leaders, most of them in charge of huge American corporations, put their success down to luck. In reality it was nothing of the kind, but it is interesting to note that the most successful leaders werc modest and happy to give credit to their colleagues.

This is the answer for you as well. If you feel embarrassed at blowing your own trumpet, then you don't need to do it. You can still make your senior manager aware of what you are doing by blowing the team's trumpet on their behalf, or by providing opportunities for them to blow it for themselves through away-day invitations to your manager or bringing team members with you to co-present your success stories or research findings.

The team get the recognition they deserve and you get the reflected glory of leading them so well that they are achieving great things under your management. By showing your team is effective and understands why it is effective, by pointing to evidence of improvement and impact, you become trusted and credible in the eyes of the most risk-averse leader. When you present your business case it will be credible too.

What if my line manager isn't very good at managing?

We have assumed so far that your challenge is to gain access to your line manager in a way that enables you to influence their thinking. Barriers to overcome are essentially time, trust and mutual understanding and that the right behaviour and the correct form of words on your part will help you to help them achieve your common goals. This is usually sufficient to enable you to make a difference and to create a good working relationship. However, it must be accepted that sometimes senior managers are not as good as they might be. When this is the case, it makes things much more difficult for both of you. In this situation it is absolutely not your job to point this out to anyone, especially the person concerned. It may make you feel better temporarily but it won't help you get what you want – and it won't do very much for your relationship with your manager either.

People become ineffective for a number of reasons, only some of which are directly down to their own aptitudes and abilities. Your line manager may not be very good with people, something that does happen if they have been promoted due to their previous performance as an accountant or engineer, in which case they weren't required to manage others. It could be that they have difficulty making decisions, perhaps because of previous experiences where their decisions backfired for them. They may have been superb in the early stages of the business as they built it up from scratch but haven't yet realised that they can't run a big enterprise in the same way as they ran a small one.

Most of us are weaker at some things than others, and it may be that you can identify your manager's strengths and weaknesses. You are in a good position to do so after all, as you have to deal with them. It's great to be an all-rounder but it can also work very well if you find a way to work with your line manager that covers all bases between you; if neither of you is particularly interested in status then you can find a way to complement each other that makes you into an effective team.

Most weaknesses, however, are either the result of organisational processes or exacerbated by them. Your position in the hierarchy should not prevent you from pointing out where processes could be improved and suggesting changes, or from involving your team in identifying and recommending changes and taking them to your line manager on their behalf. You are an important link between your team and other teams, and between your team and senior management.

The job of management is about people and process, whether at junior, middle or senior management level. Most of the problems caused by less-than-impressive senior managers can be influenced for the better, resolved or worked around by putting in place robust procedures that provide the clarity and protection that would otherwise be missing. You can suggest and, wherever possible, implement many of these procedures across the board. Have a think about the impact of decent processes for:

Meetings. Clear purpose, meaningful agendas, good use of subgroups, preparation and action points rather than lengthy minutes would all make a difference to the contribution attendees can make.

Job descriptions. Up-to-date, clearly defined roles and responsibilities (authority and limitations), agreed objectives that relate to business priorities.

Training and development. I've lost count of the number of organisations that happily book training for middle managers but not for senior leaders. If you can get senior leaders to join your team on relevant training sessions or internal workshops, it can be powerful.

Action Learning Sets. These are short sessions with small groups drawn from all levels of the organisation (sometimes including customers). They are set up to solve a specific problem or improve a key process and are a great way to pool expertise and resources by bringing together people who would not normally work closely with each other. Include your line manager in one or two of these sessions and see what happens.

Supervision and appraisal. This should be a great opportunity to increase mutual understanding, identify improvements and review agreed objectives.

Always keep the objective in mind

Management is multi-faceted: you are managing yourself, your team and, now, your manager. Oh, and your core processes, your numbers and your feedback. Easy, isn't it?

Managing your manager is another essential skill so keep it professional, don't take it personally, and try a few of the approaches outlined in this chapter. Remember, your aim is to get things done, to create an environment in which your team can perform, to represent them and to provide clear leadership. From time to time this will involve getting the best out of your own manager. They may be employed to manage you, but you are also employed to manage *them*. In doing so you'll achieve much more as a partnership, even if you know it and *they* don't!

Managing Your Manager: Takeaways from Chapter Nine

♦ Take a metaphorical walk in their shoes before judging them – you can't influence anyone without understanding what influences them

♦ Bring them solutions, not problems. They are likely to be time-starved and problems or 'whinges' are unwelcome

♦ Clarify boundaries and expectations. You need to know what you can and can't do without the need to seek their permission

♦ Don't be too modest about your achievements. Culturally, we may find it difficult to push ourselves forward and say how wonderful we are, so we don't make our line manager aware of the great work we are doing. Find a routine way of giving them the evidence – regular short reports, notes of actions taken or agreed, monitoring and feedback

♦ A track record of achievement will increase their confidence in you and help build trust

♦ Give them the opportunity to join in with specific positive events such as action learning sets or well-structured and prepared meetings with clear objectives.

10

Virtuous Circles: Keeping It Fresh and Meaningful

If it ain't broke . . .

Successful teams continually plan, review and improve. Good performance now may not be good in a few months' time, or an advantage over a competitor may no longer be an advantage unless we keep looking ahead to the next thing we can do. If handled correctly, this can be a very positive mindset. I'm not saying that we should adopt a mentality in which nothing we do is ever good enough; it is instead a mentality in which we form the habit of looking for ways to make our performance better.

In discussing change we looked at the difference between change for its own sake and change as a means to an end. The best and most motivational change will involve tweaks and improvements to fine-tune our thinking and our processes to enable us to achieve our goals and increase our impact.

Everything is a process and all processes need to be looked after in order to keep working efficiently. Your team or organisation is no exception. A car will not perform unless it has the right fuel, is properly maintained and driven well; a pot plant soon dies unless it is watered, fed and has access to light. Your team has its own needs that must be fulfilled in order for it to perform in the way you want it to and, while those needs may be more complex than a car or a pot plant, the principle is the same: you cannot expect anything to continue to do what you want it to unless you maintain it.

> *Maintenance is a continuous process. It's no good doing the things we have worked through in this book only once or twice and thinking we've done our job.*

Our relationship with our team, like any other, needs constant work and reinforcement. We need to be consistent in applying the principles and values we say we live by or those principles and values will be undermined. Our focus must sharpen as we get closer to our goals. We must continually remind ourselves of what is important and we cannot afford to compromise on our core values.

Culture and values

'Culture and values': words such as these can sometimes sound a bit over the top, can't they? After all, we're only talking about coming into work and doing whatever we do for eight hours or so and going home again. So are they really relevant? I believe they are.

I recently ran a senior management course for a group of people who work for a growing company, and who have been identified as future leaders as the organisation expands. Keen to learn, they worked hard to achieve their qualifications and contributed well in the group. They were also committed to the success of the company and took pride in their part in its achievements; they spoke about its aims, its vision and its values, using words such as 'openness', 'honesty' and 'passion'. They were full of ideas and all saw themselves staying in their roles and growing with the organisation.

What struck me most was the obvious enjoyment they had in working for their company. Their business was all about making doors and windows, and the managers were involved in sales, finance and human resources. They didn't leave school dreaming of making doors and windows, or working in sales or finance, but they loved what they were doing. Why? Because they felt they were part of something bigger than them, they felt challenged, respected and acknowledged.

When I spoke to their director I could see why: he believed in involving and stretching his staff, and he did so – consistently. The company also had a simple, clear mission statement that focused on adding value for the customer. Again, not unusual; lots of companies have similar statements. The difference here was that everyone in that session knew the mission and it came up in conversation often during the time I spent with them.

The mission statement was a genuine one; the company had structured its operation around supporting that vision and making it into the most important thing the business focused on. Everything they did was measured against that standard and judged on whether or not it would help them to deliver it. Sometimes that meant spending large sums of money; other times it meant restructuring manufacturing processes or retraining of sales staff. It affected how the finance team processed payments and how materials were ordered and stored. The mission became the company, and the company in turn became its mission.

Add to this the director's belief in investing in his staff, challenging them to set and achieve stretching targets while supporting them with coaching, training and feedback, and you will identify two words that describe pretty well what they had created: culture and values.

Culture is what we do. When we do what we say we will do, we demonstrate authenticity. People respond to that. It's not enough to say that we value our customers; we have to show that we do by actually valuing them. We can't say that we value our staff without backing that up by giving them opportunity and supporting them to take advantage of it.

These things come from the top of the organisation. If we ourselves are not at the top, then our responsibility is to demonstrate them in our own sphere of influence. If we say something is important then we need to demonstrate its importance by doing it ourselves, reinforcing the message to others, agreeing relevant actions, allocating resources to it, monitoring it and providing recognition and feedback. In so doing, we create a culture and a set of values that people can recognise and commit to. If we don't, not only is there no encouragement for anyone to help us achieve our goals but there is a disincentive as people lose faith in the project and lose trust in your message. We need to feed and water our plant to help it grow; we must maintain our car to keep it running. We need something to give our team momentum.

Standards

Working to agreed and meaningful standards is another aspect of culture and values. Standards are part of the process. If you are trying to create and maintain a set of standards they will make the most impact if they are clearly related to what you are trying to achieve. Whether it's a uniform or dress code, a set of core principles or an agreed set of behaviours, standards are an expression of your values.

We all come to work to earn money; we all need to generate profit or surplus to keep our organisation in business. How we do that is up to us. If we have a clear set of values, and our work is an extension of those values, maintaining standards becomes second nature.

Trust

Trust breeds security and confidence, which means that your team know where they stand. There needs to be an element of predictability so there are no nasty surprises such as behavioural ones (temper tantrums, mood swings, favouritism or inconsistency of any kind) or logical ones (sudden changes of direction, contradictions, lack of follow-up or removal of resources).

Trust can easily be broken or compromised, often completely by accident. We are juggling with so many different priorities that it's easy to take your eye off one of the balls and, if that happens to be something you've agreed with a colleague, you need to be aware of it and put it right.

Dr Steven Covey, author of *The 7 Habits of Highly Effective People*, has an excellent metaphor for this called the 'emotional bank account', which operates in the same way as a conventional bank account in that you make deposits and withdrawals. He argues that if you promise to do something for someone (a deposit) and then don't do it (a withdrawal), the impact of a withdrawal is more profound than a deposit, putting you in the red with your colleague. It might be as simple as promising to meet the next day to discuss something of importance to them, then not fulfilling your promise. If they feel let down, they believe that they are not as important to you as you claim. The remedy is simply to take the trouble to contact them beforehand, explain that you can't make the appointment and make another one.

Monitoring

Mention monitoring to most people and they think of tick boxes and routine checking; a boring activity often done to show others that we have done it rather than a valuable task in its own right. Monitoring is, in fact, what managers and leaders spend the vast majority of their time doing, and for good reason too.

In terms of the Tuckman stages of team development model (Forming, Storming, Norming, Performing, see also page 59), most of us are in teams that are in the performing stage. The team has been established, the objectives agreed, and the processes are in place. The team is delivering its service, manufacturing its products, selling them or otherwise fulfilling the needs of its clients or customers.

So, what do we do as the team leader? The answer is, of course, that we lead. It's not enough to sit back and watch while we turn the wheel and produce what we've always produced. We are interested in maintenance and improvement. We are looking at the results we are getting, and what we can put into the system to improve those results. We are measuring, testing, giving and receiving feedback and generating ideas. We need to know what is being done, how it is being done and how performance compares to profile. We must decide what needs measuring and reporting on to enable us to identify trends and act on them. It is also an important part of our role to obtain feedback from colleagues, customers and other relevant stakeholders.

Monitoring is an early warning system, giving us current information to enable us to steer the ship. It helps us to stay on course by alerting us to any deviation in time to make a sensible change. Monitoring is a first line of defence against future problems. If we can keep people involved in monitoring their own activities and the results they are producing as an individual and as a team, we will all perform better.

Jim Collins and his team in his book, *Good To Great*, identified the importance of keeping our focus on what we need to do in order to achieve our goal and to keep on doing it. They called this activity the 'flywheel' and argued that successful organisations continually touch the flywheel to keep it moving, and over time the flywheel gathers momentum so that the smallest touch generates ever-greater speed. Those touches work because they are the result of good information, and that information is gained by constant monitoring of processes and outcomes.

Monitoring is itself a cycle, gathering relevant data then turning it into information that we can use. If you place that information regularly in front of colleagues and stakeholders, you are then equipped to evaluate it, analysing it to enable you to form judgements about the best ways to improve what you are doing. This informs your next touch on the flywheel.

So, monitoring is great for checking progress, involving people in discussion and keeping focused. Evaluation allows you and your team or your line manager to assess what your monitoring activity is telling you and to make appropriate changes.

I was doing some consultancy work with a manager in an FE College one day when I heard the song 'Build Me Up, Buttercup' coming from a plastic pot plant on the office windowsill. It was the third time I had heard it in one morning, so I asked the manager what was going on. She told me that each time their data team entered an achievement of a qualification onto the system they had to press the plastic buttercup. Each time they heard that song, they knew another student had achieved.

Team meetings

Team meetings, and meetings in general, are one of the biggest missed opportunities in the workplace. There are all kinds of ways to waste what should be a great chance to get together as a group, pool resources and move forward. Some of my favourite ways to waste meetings are:

◆ The chair reads out information from a sheet of paper no one else has a copy of, then asks if anyone has any questions or comments

◆ Most of the meeting consists of each attendee being asked what they are currently doing, or will be doing next week

◆ No one has seen the agenda, or read it even if they have been sent it

◆ People arrive late, leave early or don't bother coming at all

◆ There is no purpose to the meeting beyond that of holding one.

My personal 'Road to Damascus' moment came when I attended no fewer than eight meetings in one day, two of which I was chairing. You can imagine how useful those meetings were and how effective my contribution was to the meetings as the day wore on.

If you want your team meetings to be useful, the first step should be to decide what you want to use them for. A meeting without a purpose shouldn't happen as it is a waste of resource that reduces efficiency and can make people either bored or resentful. A poorly planned meeting can also be a convenient place for people to bring up their pet topics in an unstructured way, making it difficult for them to identify what they want and for you to resolve it.

There are a lot of good guides to running team meetings and I don't propose to go into too much detail here (the *One Minute Manager* series by Kenneth Blanchard and Spencer Johnson covers aspects of building and leading teams, see Bibliography, page 166). The main factor I want to stress at this point is that team meetings provide an ideal opportunity to involve your team in all the positive and interesting aspects of performance. Try giving people specific responsibilities and slots in meetings to enable them to feed back to colleagues, test ideas, agree solutions and identify opportunities, then capture what you have all achieved in a clear set of agreed actions and decisions as soon after the meeting as possible. These are more effective than lengthy minutes and reinforce the idea that this is a business process with clear outcomes. It also makes follow-up and review so much easier to do.

Learning and development

Continuous learning and development goes hand in hand with continuous improvement. Self-development is essential for all kinds of reasons, and there are spin-offs in terms of the growth of the team, increased self-esteem and confidence and creating a culture of learning and challenge. There are also benefits in terms of increased capacity, career prospects and succession planning. The flow of ideas as people bring back new thinking and techniques is also invaluable.

Self-development is hugely motivating. Some organisations may find it difficult to fund external training programmes or qualifications, but there are a lot of learning opportunities that you can provide within the organisation that cost only time. These include coaching, mentoring, shadowing others, research and building in opportunities internally for one team member to cascade learning to others. Perhaps the most powerful of all is learning on the job, if you provide opportunities for people to work together to design and deliver process improvements, plan for achieving goals and building partnerships.

Last, but not at all least, make sure you as manager keep on learning too!

Stakeholders, partners and colleagues

Clients, customers and other stakeholders can be demanding but they are the reason we are in business. Wouldn't it be great if we could somehow make them part of the team instead of an extra external pressure? If we can find a way to bring them into our thinking rather than work separately from them they become an asset and can help us to keep on improving.

A stakeholder is anyone who has an interest in what we are doing and may benefit from it. Because of that they are likely to have opinions and ideas that will help us to give them what they need. There is a lot of work done by organisations to find out what customers think of their service, through online and phone questionnaires and so on, and they have their place. Personally I am more interested in how we can actively work with clients and partners to improve our service as this is what really makes a difference.

Case Study

I once led a training company that provided qualifications and back-to-work support for unemployed adults. In our regular team meetings we noticed a downward trend in the number of unemployed people joining our programmes. This had become quite marked and we knew that this would affect our profitability if we didn't do something to correct it.

We had one major partner organisation, which was the Jobcentre. They were the people referring clients to us, and we were getting fewer referrals from them each month. When I asked the team why, they said that staff turnover at the Jobcentre meant we were always dealing with someone new, who didn't know the programmes. They also said that there were other providers also offering programmes and ours looked no different to any of them.

At first sight these were issues that we couldn't control. However, to accept them meant that we were putting ourselves in the role of victims of circumstance: the causes were with the partner organisation and we couldn't affect them. So I turned the question around and asked what could we do that would help our partner to refer more people. This put the emphasis on us, not them, and we had a breakthrough moment resulting in some simple but effective action (most effective action is simple after all).

We did two things that transformed the situation, in partnership with the Jobcentre. Firstly, we placed a member of staff with them for a day a week to build relationships with their client advisers and put us at the front of their minds. They now had a face to put to a name and could ask questions about what we offered. Secondly, we realised that all they ever heard about us would be from unsuccessful clients who returned to them having failed to secure a job. So we started to proactively feed back to them whenever someone they had referred gained a qualification or a job. Referrals steadily increased and dialogue became regular and well informed.

Difficult conversations, facing up to problems and identifying opportunities are core behaviours in a winning, or improving, team. Involving stakeholders and partners can only benefit everyone.

Appraisals, supervision and catch-ups

Appraisals. Most organisations have some form of appraisal system with annual performance reviews and, usually, additional meetings throughout the year. The appraisal can be problematic, especially if tied to grading systems or performance-related pay, but should be a chance to gain clarity on anything related to personal and team performance.

Performance appraisals, done well and for the right reasons, are essential for the effective management and evaluation of staff. Appraisals help develop individuals, improve team performance and feed into business planning. A well-run appraisal system, in which individual staff and their managers play a full and active role, is an important part of effective management and team working.

Managers are often nervous about conducting appraisals, and that makes sense as any form of judgement is always going to be sensitive for the person being judged and we want to do it well. However, if you look on the appraisal process as a chance to spend quality time with your team member focusing on what is important for you as manager, them as an individual and the team as a whole then it's a great opportunity to discuss issues properly and make good, informed decisions.

A phrase I like to use to describe appraisals is 'looking back in order to look forwards'. We can't do anything about what has already happened so there is no point in endlessly revisiting it, but we must acknowledge it and we can learn from it. At the end of a good, well-prepared and structured appraisal discussion you will both know exactly what you have agreed and what you will be doing next. It's an important part of the time you should be spending with your team and can and should be a way to develop and improve working relationships.

An appraisal should never be a one-off event, but part of a continuous process, drawing on evidence and conversations held throughout the year.

The appraisal meeting is not just about the individual's performance; it is also about their role within the team and wider organisation, and about their own perception of their performance. There are also some more essential housekeeping considerations to get right in planning the meeting; they may seem a little basic but I remember being driven to a meeting by my manager and discussing a few work issues before being told on arrival, 'That was your appraisal, is that OK? Only I haven't had time to do it so far.' We got on well, worked together successfully and he was pleased with my work but I think it's worth taking the time to have an actual meeting.

Conventional wisdom tells you that this is the appraisee's meeting and represents their chance to have their say. That's true, of course, but I think it is also your meeting and an opportunity for you to address things that you need to resolve. An HR manager recently told me that one of her most senior managers had just completed an appraisal for a particularly problematic manager. This individual was at the centre of a number of complaints about his communication skills, but none of these were discussed in his appraisal, which was glowing in all areas. This is unfair on the manager, who is left unable to tackle his own difficulties, the staff who work for that manager, and the HR team who are left picking up the pieces.

Supervisions, 1–1 meetings and catch-ups. However your organisation arranges its performance review process, or even if they don't have one at all, regular 1–1 meetings are hard to do without. Even in a small team where we see someone every day, it is still worth spending time with that person discussing their role, their contribution and their place in the team.

We don't want our only conversations about performance to be a formal annual appraisal any more than we want them to be snatched conversations as we pass in the corridor. There is no substitute for focused attention on each member of the team, with an opportunity for you both to raise issues, recognise their achievements and plan ahead for any short-term goals. A regular twenty minutes every few weeks is a small commitment to make in order to build and maintain good working relationships.

Coaching. A coaching relationship is a great approach for developing team members, reinforcing key messages and building confidence and understanding. The role of a coach is to allow staff to stretch themselves by trying new skills, tools and techniques in a safe way, with the support and advice of a more experienced person and without the fear of negative consequences if they don't get it right first time.

Avoid 'mission drift'

We have seen throughout this journey from doubt and anxiety to security and success that one of the most effective ways to keep momentum is to focus on our goal. If the goal or mission is really the most important thing we are working towards then it should drive our decision-making.

As soon as we allow ourselves to lose that commitment to our mission we lose the sense of being engaged in something coherent and meaningful. It is easy to be blown off-course in responding to the latest challenge or indeed the latest fad or theory. It is also easy to chase markets or money that we are either not suited for or that don't fit in with our mission and values. This is 'mission drift', which causes our energy and sense of purpose to dissipate in chasing short-term goals instead of long-term ones.

Turning down appealing but irrelevant activity in favour of long-term agreed objectives is a strength that only a confident and focused team is strong enough to do.

Celebrate achievement

People are goal-driven and we work best if we feel we are working for a purpose. We enjoy belonging to something bigger than ourselves and a good workplace can give us that sense of being part of a shared experience. The biggest motivator of all is working with others in a shared enterprise to achieve a worthwhile goal and feeling that, in achieving it, we are making a difference.

We need to know what success looks like, and when we achieve it, we seek acknowledgement of our efforts and recognition of our achievement. Motivation is personal and it pays to get to know your team as individuals to find out what is important to them, just as it is equally important to get to know yourself well enough to find out the same about you.

There are some generic aspects of motivation that help us to keep improving and responding to challenges. Motivation is positive: we are motivated more by moving towards something than away from it. Fear may motivate for a short time but avoiding pain is only part of the story. Seeking pleasure by identifying something worth achieving and planning, discussing, overcoming problems and resolving them on the way to delivery is much more positive.

If a goal is worth achieving then it's worth celebrating. Nothing demotivates us more than thinking that what we are working on is not recognised or valued. Similarly, nothing empowers us more than being part of a winning team or a team that is demonstrably moving in the right direction. When you achieve a goal, acknowledge it; whether that's by buying a cake, holding an event, personally thanking everyone involved or playing 'Build Me Up, Buttercup' from a plastic plant pot. Find out what works for the people who helped you achieve it and provide it for them.

Then, once you've celebrated reaching your goal, agree the next one. Enjoy the journey, the experience and the sense of shared achievement. Enjoy learning from it and doing things you once thought were too hard to do. Then enjoy stretching yourself, facing forwards and doing it all again. It's up to you: you're the boss!

Management starts with you.

Virtuous Circles: Keeping It Fresh and Meaningful: Takeaways from Chapter Ten

♦ Reinforce culture, values and standards: these are only as good as current practice allows them to be

♦ Monitor all aspects of performance continuously, but do so in an open and inclusive way so you include your team in both information gathering and interpretation

♦ Everything in management is a cycle; we should be in a continuous pattern of planning, doing and reviewing, with the aim being increasing involvement and improving performance

♦ Regular and relevant team meetings, 1–1s and effective appraisals should all contribute towards a positive cycle of improvement

♦ Challenging but achievable targets ensure that we are looking forwards not backwards, and guard against complacency or boredom

♦ Remember, learning and development are continuous

♦ Celebrate successes as soon as they are achieved and agree the next worthwhile target straight away

Bibliography

Dr Eric Berne, *Games People Play: The Psychology of Human Relationships* (Penguin, 2010).

Kenneth H. Blanchard and Spencer Johnson, *The One Minute Manager* (William Morrow, 2003).

— *The New One Minute Manager* (HarperCollins, 2015).

Mike Bourne and Pippa Bourne, *Balanced Scorecard in a Week* (Hodder & Stoughton, 2000).

Mike Brearley, *The Art of Captaincy* (Hodder & Stoughton, 1985).

Jack Canfeld, *Self-Esteem and Peak Performance* (CareerTrack audio album).

Jim Collins, *Good to Great: Why Some Companies Make the Leap – and Others Don't* (Random House Business, 2001).

Dr Stephen Covey, *The 7 Habits of Highly Effective People: Powerful Lessons in Personal Change* (DC Books, 2005).

Michael E. Gerber, *The E-Myth Revisited: Why Most Small Businesses Don't Work and What to Do About It* (HarperBusiness, 2001).

— *E-Myth Mastery: The Seven Essential Disciplines for Building a World Class Company* (HarperBusiness, 2007).

Susan Jeffers, *Feel the Fear and Do It Anyway: How to Turn Your Fear and Indecision into Confidence and Action* (Vermilion, 2007).

Professor Steve Peters, *The Chimp Paradox: The Mind Management Programme to Help You Achieve Success, Confidence and Happiness* (Vermilion, 2012).

Roger Plant, *Managing Change and Making It Stick* (Fontana/Collins, 1987).

Matthew Syed, *Bounce: The Myth of Talent and the Power of Practice* (Fourth Estate, 2011).

Index

Coaching Skills for Leaders in the Workplace Revised Edition

How to unlock potential and maximise performance

Jackie Arnold

Available to buy in ebook and paperback

As a leader, senior manager or executive, you are often called on to act as coach or mentor to your staff. This book will enable you to set up the coaching programmes that will make a significant difference to your organisation.

You will discover how to:

- Present a business case for coaching, by understanding how you can use coaching programmes to enhance behaviours and retain key staff.

- Become an effective leader and coach.

- This book supports the requirements for the ILM and CMI Coaching and Mentoring in Management Qualifications at levels 5 to 7.

COACHING
SKILLS FOR
LEADERS
IN THE
WORKPLACE

How to Unlock Potential
and Maximise Performance

JACKIE ARNOLD

How To Be Confident and Assertive at Work

Practical tools and techniques that you can put into use immediately

Suzanne and Conrad Potts

Available to buy in ebook and paperback

Practical solutions for the everyday challenges of daily working life

This book gives you practical, straightforward advice and actual words to use when dealing with situations that the average person finds difficult to handle.

Like a good friend, it will enable you to be valued for who you are, to ask for what you are entitled to, and to say 'no' when you have the right to do so. You will be able to stand up for yourself and handle difficult situations calmly and successfully, and you will discover how to have your opinions and ideas heard and respected.

It provides step-by-step guidance on how to deal with the most common situations and issues that you are likely to face during your working life – including speaking at meetings and presentations, managing other people and your boss, handling appraisals and interviews, and even asking for a pay rise!

Suzanne and Conrad Potts

HOW TO BE
CONFIDENT
AND
ASSERTIVE
AT WORK

Practical tools and techniques that you can put into use immediately

THE

IMPR⟳VEMENT

ZONE

Looking for life inspiration?

The Improvement Zone has it all, from **expert advice** on how to advance your **career**, improve your **relationships**, boost your **business**, revitalise your **health** or develop your **mind**. Whatever your goals, head to our website now.